The World
in My Camera

The World in My Camera

Gisèle Freund

Translated by JUNE GUICHARNAUD

THE DIAL PRESS　New York | 1974

Library of Congress Cataloging in Publication Data

Freund, Gisèle.
  The world in my camera.

  Translation of Le Monde et ma caméra.
  I. Title.
TR140.F69A313   770'.92'4   72–1061

Grateful acknowledgment is made to the following for permission
to reprint copyrighted material:

Harcourt Brace Jovanovich, Inc.: For material adapted from *James
    Joyce in Paris*, Copyright © 1965 by Gisèle Freund.

The Society of Authors, on behalf of the Bernard Shaw Estate: For
    part of a letter by G. B. Shaw.

First published in French under the title *Le Monde et Ma Camera* by
    Denoël/Gonthier. Copyright © 1970 by Gisèle Freund.

To Marie Rodell

Contents

Illustrations

Preface

Photographs have come to play an overpowering role in our society. They are familiar to us before we learn to read and write. They illustrate our schoolbooks; our teen-agers tack them to the walls of their bedrooms. They enter our homes daily on television. They overflow albums and fill drawers by the millions. We see them in shopwindows, subways, trains, and buses, stare at them in newspapers and magazines. Photographs speak a language understood by everyone everywhere in the world.

The specific technique of taking photographs—the exact reproduction of our outer world as it appears to the eye—invests them with an aura of truth. Their apparent objectivity is cleverly exploited by those who want to sell us goods and ideas. But therein lies their ambiguity, for the same picture may be interpreted in different ways depending on how it is presented.

The technique of photography is no longer any problem, but the image recorded is still determined by the person who stands behind the camera and presses the button.

I have been a photo-reporter and portraitist for over thirty years. I have worked for the greatest and the smallest magazines, and have photographed many famous personalities. My goal has

3

4 been to make my camera a witness of the time in which I live.

In this book I recall my own experiences and at the same time try to analyze some lesser-known aspects of the photographic image and its impact on our contemporary world.

1

Flight to Freedom

I was born and raised in Berlin, where my parents had always lived. My father, a tall, handsome, blue-eyed businessman, had a passion for art. He was a collector, and the walls of our house were covered with paintings. In spite of his martial, Prussian bearing and his Wilhelm II moustache, he was a kind and gentle man with great knowledge and wit.

My mother—tiny, dark-haired, and black-eyed—was lively and active, strong and determined. My family could trace their ancestors back many generations and considered themselves good and law-abiding Germans. My upbringing was what I consider today puritanical, with strong emphasis on ethical principles and the spiritual tradition of Western civilization. Yet religion and race were never discussed in our house. I was never faced with such problems until Hitler.

In the late twenties Berlin was the center of avant-garde literature and art in Germany. I was then a teen-ager, but the theatre of Piscator and the first plays of Brecht left a lasting impression on me. As a young student, I was drawn to the liberal groups at Frankfurt University, where I studied sociology and art. When Hitler's revolution started in the early months of 1933 and Nazi terror swept over Germany, I naturally joined those who tried to oppose them.

I shall always remember a night in May 1933. Although it was more than thirty years ago, every detail is engraved on my mind. I was a healthy girl of twenty, and my chestnut hair hung down to my shoulders: I was wearing a very simple skirt and a brown suede jacket when I arrived at the railroad station that night. There was almost no one on the platform; not many people were traveling then. The few passengers were rushing to board the Paris express. The night was rainy, and as I walked up to the train, I heard the sound of heavy boots striking the wet stones. I could see, as I climbed into one of the cars, the profiles of two uniformed SS men outlined in the shadows. My heart began to beat violently. "If only they don't notice me!" I thought.

The third-class cars were almost empty. I chose a compartment in which a man of about fifty was sitting near the window. His felt hat was pulled down over his eyes, and in the dim light he seemed half asleep. I closed the door as quietly as possible, put my small suitcase up on the rack, and sat down facing him, my camera beside me. I looked at my watch; the train was to leave in a few minutes. The silence intensified my fear. Then suddenly came the dreaded sounds: tramping boots, shrill voices. They were opening the doors of compartments, asking questions. It seemed to me that the face of the man watching me from across the compartment was changing strangely in the shadows.

The door of the compartment snapped open and an SS man entered. The cold night air swept in with him and I shivered.

"Your papers," he said.

He merely glanced at those held out by the man; then, turning to me, he took my passport and slowly began to leaf through it.

"Student? Where are you going?"

"I'm returning to Paris to study."

I did my best to speak in a noncommittal and innocuous way, adding: "I'll be back in three months."

Undecided, he continued leafing through the pages. Suddenly he looked at me: "You're a Jew?"

"Have you ever heard of a Jew called Gisèle?"

I had almost shouted, in an indignant tone, imitating the authoritarian voice of my father. I looked the Nazi straight in the eye. He was not much older than I. Surprised, he returned my passport, clicked his heels, and raised his right arm: "Heil Hitler!" The door closed behind him; his footsteps grew fainter. A few seconds later the train started. I fell back in my seat, dazed. Everything had happened at dizzying speed.

That morning, in the Mainzer Landstrasse, I had met a city employee who knew me by sight. He had stopped me and whispered: "Leave, leave at once; they want to arrest all of you tonight."

He must have read the mimeographed newspaper that my student group was printing and distributing clandestinely at the university. We had violently attacked the new regime. In our last issue we had published the names of all professors who had been dismissed, and had written of the tragic fate of our friend Anne. Two weeks after her arrest, her body had reached her parents in a coffin. They had been forbidden to open it. In the darkness I remembered her pale complexion, her high, curved forehead, her silky blond hair, which she wore up, and her still childish mouth. She was only two years older than I. I had always admired her courage and intelligence. Behind a frail and feminine exterior she possessed a strong will. She had probably refused to give our names.

"You must leave," said Karl, the leader of our little group. "Your photos must cross the border so that everybody will know what is happening in our country." I had photographed the bodies of fellow students who had been beaten up by the SS.

The train picked up speed, and I let myself be lulled by its rhythm. Nothing much was discernible outside. Raindrops dripped down the windowpane, one after another, like the tears I should have liked to shed.

What good was our resistance? They had every means to destroy us. I suddenly felt weary and discouraged. It was cold

8 in the badly heated train. Through my closed eyelids I imagined the expression on the face of the man across from me, still silent and impenetrable.

And what if they made me open my camera? I was overcome with fear. Under the impassive eye of the unknown man I left the compartment, went to the lavatory, and locked the door. I opened my camera, threw the roll of film into the toilet, then returned to my seat and dozed off.

I was awakened by the train jolting to a stop. It was the border. Interminable minutes; then, again the noise of boots, the banging of doors. Immigration, passports.

"Do you have anything to declare?"

The man who asked me the question was not a customs officer in uniform but a man in plain clothes: Gestapo. Beside him stood an SS man. The customs officer himself remained at the door, vague, passive. Again I was asked for my papers, and the Gestapo agent gestured to me to take down my suitcase. He searched it thoroughly and discovered the camera.

"Open it." With a suspicious look he turned it upside down and shook it; when he was absolutely certain there was no film in it, he returned it to me. Was he going to search me? No; he walked out, followed by the others. The most important film, the film for which I had just risked my life, was hidden on me.*

When the train started again, I looked out the window. On the platform the policemen were taking away a man and woman they had just pulled off the train. Suddenly I began to feel faint. My traveling companion, who was now wide awake, looked at me. He had taken off his hat, and his eyes, peering out of a wrinkled face, were observing me compassionately.

"You have nothing to fear anymore," he said with a thick Bavarian accent. "The border is behind us."

"I'm not afraid. Why would I be afraid?" I answered defensively. At the same moment I thought: "Will I ever see my

*The photographs appeared in *Le Livre brun* in 1933 and were reproduced throughout the world.

friends again?'' They were meeting that night at the exit of the Hauptwache cinema. Was it possible that someone had denounced us? If so, which of us was the traitor? I found such an assumption inconceivable. And as for me, sitting in a train taking me toward an unknown destiny, I wondered how I would live in Paris. What would my parents say when they learned I had left? They would not understand my decision. They regarded the Nazis with disdain, but like so many other bourgeois who led a peaceful and protected existence, they never imagined that the new regime would have an influence on their own destinies.

At dawn the train was rolling through the suburbs of Paris. It was six o'clock in the morning when we arrived at the Gare du Nord. I had no way of knowing that all my friends had been arrested and that I would never again live in the country of my birth.

2

Paris in the Thirties

Paris seemed a haven of peace after the weeks I had just lived through. Apparently no one had any idea of what was going on in Germany; no one knew anything about the brutality of the new regime, the concentration camps, the persecutions. The first refugees were just beginning to arrive.

I settled down in a small hotel on the rue Saint-Julien-le-Pauvre; from my window I could gaze at the towers of Notre-Dame directly across the Seine.

Sprawled out in front was a heap of rubbish that was subsequently turned into a pretty little park. But at the time no one was much concerned with "that square patch," as Colette used to call it, swarming with indigent craftsmen, students, loose women, bistros and dance halls, stray dogs and cats. During the day it resounded with the clatter of wagons passing along the Seine, and at night one's ears were filled with the din from the Caveau des Oubliettes, where old French songs were sung into the small hours. The air stank from the fat used by a vendor of french fries, which would simmer on a little stove in front of his door. Behind the square, on the corner of the rue Lagrange and the rue de Fouarre, was a bar where the *clochards* could spend

Caveau des Oubliettes

the night when it was too cold under the bridges of the Seine. For twenty centimes the owner would hang a loop of rope from the ceiling so that a man could rest his head on it as he slept.

The grimy, dilapidated houses on my street seemed ready to collapse at any moment. A wooden scaffolding supported the last two; to walk between them, you had to bend down so as not to bump your head on the beam.

My room was no different from hundreds of other hotel rooms in the Latin Quarter, worn out by generations of students. The walls were covered with a greenish paper, decorated with faded red tulips. The furniture consisted of an iron bed, a table, and an old plush armchair. It was in that setting that I made my first experiments as a photographer. I never learned the profession at a school. Like millions of other amateurs, I took pictures as instructed by the camera manufacturers' slogan: "Just press the button; we'll do the rest."

I soon discovered that the amateur can develop film himself without any great training. I transformed my washstand, hidden behind a curtain, into a darkroom by setting my tank on a board placed over the sink and my enlarger on the bidet.

The owner of the hotel looked upon these transformations with a distrustful eye. He was probably afraid that his old arm-

Rue Saint-Julien-le-Pauvre

Paris street

14 chair would be damaged by my developers. But when I did a portrait of his daughter, he was mollified.

I enrolled at the Sorbonne to take courses in sociology and worked across from the Panthéon, at the Sainte-Geneviève Library, which James Joyce had often used early in the century. With students constantly coming and going, and talking to each other from one table to another, it was difficult to concentrate: Sainte-Geneviève was a real hen house.

At noon I ate at a dairy restaurant on the rue de la Huchette, along with other students and people who worked in the neighborhood. All the regular customers had their own napkins in numbered pigeonholes.

Sometimes, to save money, I made do with a sandwich. I would pass the Petit Pont, the parvis of Notre-Dame, and, walking beyond the Hôtel-Dieu on my left, would sit on a bench in the garden overlooking the Seine. There I often met an old lady who walked her cat on a leash.

"Minou needs a little sun," she told me. "Animals need fresh air just as we do."

After having settled her cat in a basket on the grass, she would open her worn handbag and take out a pair of steel-rimmed glasses and a small book. Now and then she would look up from her reading and cast a vigilant eye on the animal sleeping at her feet.

Afterward, walking along the quays, I would watch the *clochards* stretched out in the sun, all in tatters, yet clearly cautious: they had taken good care to stretch out on newspapers to protect themselves from the damp. Beside them you could see the baby carriages in which they carried all their worldly goods. Now and then barges would sail down the river, leaving trails of smoke that merged with the bluish gray of the sky. The secondhand bookstalls seemed to grow out of the parapets; I often rummaged in the stands filled with old buttons, postcards, music scores, and ancient coins. Engravings and prints, attached with safety pins, fluttered in the breeze.

I had chosen to write my thesis on the history of photography in the nineteenth century, for in the process of taking photo-

The Latin Quarter

The old lady with the cat

graphs, many questions about the invention of the camera itself had occurred to me. The books dealing with its history were mostly technical. No one had yet studied photography in its relation to the social aspects of the period in which it had originated—that is, vis-à-vis the rise of the middle class in nineteenth-century France. These new social strata needed their own forms of expression—forms that corresponded to their tastes and means. The invention of photography made it possible for them to possess and transmit their own image at little cost.

The Sainte-Geneviève Library was soon inadequate to my research and I changed to the National Library on the rue de Richelieu. The atmosphere there was very different. A glazed dome, through which filtered a diffused gray light, covered the much larger reading room. Most of the readers were regular visitors. Scientists, researchers, journalists, and erudite monks worked side by side with deputies who came to write their speeches. The air smelled of dust and of a sweetish disinfectant that a guard sprayed around from time to time. Everyone worked in deep silence.

At ten minutes to five the closing of the library was announced by a guard. A few moments before the official signal, a kind of shrill cry, ending in a long barking cough, reverberated through the room. A guard told me that the little bearded old man, all stooped over, who emitted that sound had done the same every day for nearly ten years.

"He always has the same book on insects brought to him; he's a bit deranged, but since he doesn't harm anybody, we let him stay."

I had as a neighbor a distinguished old gentleman with a long white moustache; from time to time he would fall asleep and his snoring gave a strange rhythm to the silence.

In fine weather I would walk home through the arcade of the Palais-Royal and linger in front of the windows of tiny shops that specialized in selling flamboyant ribbons, decorations, commemorative medals, and postage stamps. A provincial calm reigned in the gardens. Colette had not yet moved in.

Clochards

At the end of the day I sometimes went to Montparnasse to pick up a friend who was posing for a painter. The Dôme, the Coupole, and the Rotonde were then the real centers of the artistic and literary avant-garde, well before Saint-Germain-des-Près came into vogue. Everyone would meet at these sidewalk cafés. Picasso, surrounded by friends, was already considered the greatest painter of his generation. The surrealists were grouped around André Breton; in his brown corduroy jacket, with blond wavy hair almost touching his shoulders, he looked like an apostle. At another table was a circle of admirers around Léon-Paul Fargue, who was to become a friend of mine a few years later. Kiki, the famous model of the Japanese painter Foujita, as well as of Kisling and many others, was also a regular customer of the Dôme. Young painters just starting out would

OPPOSITE PAGE. *The National Library* LEFT. *A National Library reader at closing time* BELOW. *My companion at the library*

walk among the tables and offer to do portraits of the customers for a few francs.

At the National Library I often met Walter Benjamin, the German writer and essayist. Sometimes we would leave together at the end of the day and play chess in a corner café. He committed suicide in June 1940. Fleeing the German invasion of France, he was arrested by Spanish guards while trying to cross the border. He feared they would hand him over to the Gestapo. Today his essays on literature and art are considered among the most important works of the period.

I had a keen interest in literature. It was an exceptional period. The beginning of the thirties saw several generations of brilliant writers all living in France. Their world was dominated by three great names: Valéry, Claudel, and Gide.

It was at the National Library that I met Alix Guillain, companion of the philosopher and writer Bernard Groethuysen, who in literary circles was nicknamed Socrates. He was extremely wise and subtle and possessed a vast store of knowledge. It was through him that so many great foreign writers, such as Kafka, became known in France.

It was thanks to the Groethuysens that I made my first contact with the literary circles of Paris. They introduced me to Jean Paulhan, editor of the *Nouvelle Revue Française*. Every Wednesday he would receive his friends in his office on the rue Sébastien-Bottin, which is still the home of the review. Paulhan, with his curiously sardonic wit, was the dominant figure at those gatherings. I always found something diabolical about his face: his thick eyebrows jutted out over delicate brown eyes, subtle and full of irony. His gentle, high voice was in singular contrast to his massive body. He was considered the *éminence grise* of French letters.

One afternoon on the terrace of Paulhan's office, I encountered André Gide, with his clean-shaven ascetic face, talking to a young romantic-looking man.

Walter Benjamin, 1937

Jean Paulhan, 1937

22

"You must meet André Malraux," Paulhan told me. "Gide, who is very infatuated with revolutionary ideas, considers him his spiritual son."

Malraux was then about thirty. His anxious eyes darted from one person to another, from object to object, like a hunted bird seeking refuge. Gesticulating, he would break into a kind of vehement pantomime. His simplest words conveyed a sense of drama. And, with his cigarette butt stuck to his lip, he talked tirelessly.

It was also at one of those gatherings that I met Paul Valéry, Jules Supervielle, and Henri Michaux. Michaux was still unknown to the public, although the *NRF* had published several of his works. He looked extremely shy. I was struck by the strange and remote expression in his eyes.

Henri
Michaux,
1938

3

Suicide in the Seine

Fall was moving swiftly into winter. The weather was turning cold. The trees in the Luxembourg Garden had lost their leaves, and hot-chestnut vendors were taking over the street corners. In front of the cafés, oyster stands had replaced the tables. It was during this time that I witnessed one of those obscure tragedies that are so frequent in big cities like Paris.

It had rained the whole night. The muddy water of the Seine had risen a great deal during the last few days and was flowing furiously. I was crossing the Pont des Arts when I noticed a group of passersby bending over the parapet. They were watching two men in a small boat berthed at the quay. I saw them lift up what seemed to me a heavy bundle of wet clothing. As they carefully placed it on the ground, a policeman rushed over. I joined the group that had gathered. It was a girl. She appeared to be sleeping the weary sleep of an unhappy child. Long blond curls floated around a face frozen into a sort of ultimate challenge. She was wearing a white blouse and a short black skirt. But what caught my horrified eyes were her black shoes with their excessively high heels, the water running out of them drop by drop.

I don't recall having taken out my camera, but suddenly it was in my hands; I had taken a photograph. I then hastily moved away. What was the secret of that silent figure? Poverty? An unhappy love affair? I never knew, but the image of those black shoes with their ridiculous heels, dripping water from the Seine, has never left me. Mixed in with other images in the kaleidoscope of my life, it has constantly risen to the surface, perhaps out of a sense of guilt that the dead girl should have given me my first opportunity to earn my living as a photographer.

The money my parents sent me by roundabout ways (the Nazi administration having forbidden any remittance of funds to foreign countries) reached me irregularly and was barely enough for me to live on. A friend suggested that I sell my photographs. As a student at the Ecole des Beaux-Arts, he had to pay for his studies by writing short news reports for a daily paper. "Stray cats," he said, laughing.

"Look, give me the picture of the unknown beauty fished out of the Seine. Maybe my boss will publish it."

I hesitated, for the photograph was not very good.

"It doesn't matter. Lend it to me for a day and we'll see."

His optimism was contagious, but I remained skeptical. The idea of making a profession of photography had not yet occurred to me. The next evening he returned in great excitement and placed a ten-franc note on the table.

"There," he said, smiling proudly. "The boss thinks your picture's pretty bad, but he found the subject interesting."

It was an extraordinary event. Unexpected prospects opened out before me. Thus I began my career as a professional photographer, while at the same time continuing my studies.

4

My First Clients

In the early days of photography the number of professionals was considerably limited by technical difficulties. Moreover, photography was so enveloped in mystery that it acquired a special aura of artistic creation. But then, when small, portable, inexpensive cameras came on the market, the world began to swarm with amateurs. The camera was soon as indispensable to Sunday outings as the walking stick. Parallel to this technical evolution came an evolution in art. Amateurs began to compete with professionals, especially in portraiture. While the professional photographer was more than ever dependent on the often questionable taste of his clients, the amateur was free of such constraints. Unacquainted with what by then constituted a whole body of traditions and conventions, unaware of retouching, and with neither a studio nor props at his disposal, he had to strive for harmony between the faces he was photographing and the natural world. Indeed, the outdoor portrait opened a new era for photography.

The best portraits during the first decades of the twentieth century were the work of amateurs. The profound changes that had taken place were even more noticeable in the taking of children's portraits, which involved such strong feelings. There was no longer any question of retouching, and naturalness prevailed over artificiality. In fact, the avant-garde movement that developed between the two world wars originated in large part from amateur photography.

This return to a new realism was closely bound up with the political tendencies of the day. In America writers such as Sinclair Lewis, Upton Sinclair, Hemingway, Steinbeck, and others were tending toward a rigorous and documentary realism that reflected their reaction to the brutality of American life. They were often reproached for their "photographic style." In Germany the *Neue Sachlichkeit* movement was responsible for a new trend in art, expressed in a style devoid of embellishments, especially in decoration. In France the surrealist movement related real facts of life to unconscious drives. The new reality of Soviet life was recorded on film, most particularly in the works of Eisenstein. As for journalism, reporters began writing stories on the actual life of the man in the street. The public was demanding facts.

In the thirties certain photographers moved toward a deliberate realism: reproducing only a head, they ruthlessly immortalized every blemish on the skin, enlarging details. They would make no more concessions to the public; they would obtain portraits that were natural, above all. They were the avowed enemies of posing.

I felt myself deeply attracted to these new art movements. In Germany I had already been acquainted with the works of the Bauhaus and the photographs of Moholy-Nagy. In Paris, Man Ray was at the height of his fame. When I heard that he gave lessons, I went to see him. But the price he asked was as much as I lived on for a month and I had to give up the idea of being his pupil. Many decades later, when we had become friends, we laughed about it together. I went to meetings of the surrealists and read their manifestos. Photography played an important role in their activities. I was present at the first viewing of Buñuel's film *Un Chien andalou*, shown in the avant-garde cinema Studio 28 in Montmartre, which produced a stormy protest from the spectators, who bombarded the screen with eggs and tomatoes. I had become friendly with a group of young people of my age who were ardent followers of the modern art movements. We met frequently on the café-terraces of boulevard Saint-Michel, talking for hours over a cup of coffee. We had in common our enthusiasm and our poverty.

The doorman of my hotel spread the news that I was willing to do portraits for a very reasonable fee. Soon I became known among the tradesmen in my neighborhood. My shoemaker, whose young wife had just had a fat baby, asked me to photograph it; the laundress on the block wanted a photo of her son, a soldier on leave.

It was not easy to make a natural portrait. It was even more difficult to satisfy clients with my idea of realism.

The wine seller on the street, Monsieur Durand, was almost six feet, six inches tall, had small black eyes, large red ears, and a Gaullish moustache. One day, as I was buying a bottle of red wine, he bent over the counter and whispered:

"My wife has been asking for my portrait for years. Are you expensive? Business isn't so good these days."

His shop, filled with huge barrels and hundreds of bottles, reeked of vinegary wine. No Frenchman ever eats without also drinking a glass of wine. But even if business is thriving, it's advisable to complain.

"Not expensive at all, Monsieur. And if you like, we can make an exchange. You give me a few bottles of wine, and I'll make you a fine portrait; in fact, if you're not pleased with it, you won't owe me anything."

When he arrived at my place, Durand was wearing a superb tie and was dressed up like someone's best man.

"Sit down, Monsieur; are you comfortable? Would you like a small cushion on your chair?"

"Not at all, not at all, I'm fine."

He looked around him with curiosity. But as soon as he saw the eye of the camera fixed on his face, he began to stiffen.

"Be natural; I won't hurt you. Smoke a cigarette. Would you like to listen to the radio? Or would you prefer me to put on a record of Maurice Chevalier?"

Monsieur Durand, too busy watching me prepare my lamps,

did not hear a word I said. The room was dark and I had to use strong bulbs. My client was obviously hot.

"Do the lights bother you?"

"Not a bit," he lied, mopping his brow.

"What do you think about the cost of living?"

Quite a lot, probably, but that subject, which at any other time would have fascinated Durand, no longer interested him; nothing could divert his attention from the small black hole placed in front of him.

"I feel like I do at the dentist's," he finally admitted, looking at me anxiously. He was obviously tormented by doubt.

"I promise to pay very careful attention to your cheeks and nose, Monsieur. I agree that your right profile is better than your left."

"Don't you think I should undo the top button of my jacket? It would make me more comfortable."

"That's a fine idea."

For a while my model was fully occupied with changing his position, turning his head, looking down, then up; in short, he was cooperating.

The time passed. Monsieur Durand, who deemed that the sitting was over, got up. Despair! It was at that very moment that I was finally going to begin photographing him. Disillusioned, he sank back in his chair, no longer bothered about posing or about his expression. I finally had him as I wanted him: natural.

"Ah no, that's not my husband; I don't want those portraits; throw them in the fire. You don't know your job!"

Madame Durand was indignant.

"That *is* your husband, Madame."

Couldn't she see that I had even improved on him? What did she want? It wasn't my fault that he had a double chin and pig's eyes with pouches under them, or that his face was bloated from tasting wine all day.

Madame Durand glanced at me defiantly, threw the prints on the counter, and turned her back on me. I had stopped existing for her.

Portrait photography, as it was conceived by a few photog-

raphers in the thirties, was doomed from the very beginning as
a means of livelihood. The most courageous men cannot bear
to see themselves as they are. When we look into a mirror, we
see not only our features but our personalities, our characters,
and we have an unfortunate tendency to idealize ourselves. The
image we have of ourselves is more psychological than physical;
that is one of the reasons we are almost always disappointed by
our photographs.

To earn a living in portrait photography, it was necessary
to retouch in order to beautify the model. If one was able to
make one's clients resemble movie stars—that is, endow them
with a fashionable type of beauty—one's success was assured.
For those who refused to comply, the only alternative was to
photograph their friends, or artists and writers, who were ever
ready for new experiences. But if a photographer wanted to
make a living as well, he had to turn to other branches of the
profession—reporting or advertising.

5

The Ethics
of Photo-Reporting

In May 1968, during the student rebellion in France, I was
invited by the students at the National School of Photography
to take part in their meetings. An unparalleled wave of self-
criticism had taken hold of French youth and was stirring up the
entire educational system. The red flag was floating over the
Sorbonne, and discussions were taking place in lecture halls day
and night. The photography students had also occupied their
school on the rue de Vaugirard. I was one of twenty experienced
photographers they had asked for advice on modernizing the
two-year course. They were concerned as well about the fact
that, out of school, they had trouble finding jobs, especially
since all of them were ambitious to become photo-reporters.

Today the profession has acquired an aura of glory. The
photo-reporter has become a kind of star who, in twenty-four
hours, can confer celebrity on anyone, should the photographs
appear in one of the big picture magazines. His career is a
subject for films. He is thought to make enormous sums of
money traveling all over the world; he mingles with the great
men of the day.

On September 21, 1968, the newspaper *Le Monde* printed

the following advertisement, under a picture of a camera mounted on a tripod beside a suitcase filled with photographic equipment:

TAKE THE PHOTOGRAPHER'S PLACE

Yes, come on in. He left Paris last night for Marrakesh: backgrounds for a great dress designer . . . a hundred pounds of excess luggage: two Hasselblads and Nikons with every kind of lens, two Polaroids for trial shots, reflectors, accessories, dresses, his suits. . . .

He's spending a week out there with Sammy (his chief assistant), Ulla, Charlène, Doris. . . . The September light is beautiful in the dunes and palm groves.

Then he'll go to London, the Camargue, Hamburg, Scotland, Paris again, and the studio. That's what you're dreaming of, isn't it? You find his job attractive; you envy the life he leads; his success and his fame fascinate you.

Well, we at the X School in Paris say to you in all seriousness: you will be a photographer in a year! If you are young, ambitious, and dynamic, if you *really love* photos and if you're "eager," our correspondence course, "The Art of Photography," is meant for you: twelve exciting volumes. . . . And in one year you will no longer be taking the photographer's place . . . you'll be making a place for yourself!

I wonder what the students at the photography school thought of that.

It is true that in our civilization of images, photography has come to play a dominant role. People are reading less and less, but seeing more and more—hence the growing importance of photo-reporting as a profession. However, all those who, like me, have worked in the trade know that it is not easy and is often thankless. The illusion created by the ad in *Le Monde* is fascinating; the reality is something else. Even if a photographer does a fine story, he still must find a newspaper to publish it, or if he is employed by a magazine, he must bow to the demands of the editor. If he is lucky enough to see his photos reproduced, he may well not recognize them, for everything depends on how

32   they are presented. I had an experience of this kind at the very beginning of my career.

"A good reporter," I was told by a friend who worked on the staff of an illustrated paper, "must manage to take sensational photographs anywhere. Imagine yourself within the four walls of a prison cell. If you have a good eye, you'll manage to do a thrilling story."

I confess that I hardly felt encouraged.

On my way to the National Library I sometimes passed near the Stock Exchange. One day, intrigued by the clamor coming from there, I walked over. Armed with my Leica, I drew near the arcade and mixed with the crowd listening to the brokers' bids, while quotations were written on a blackboard behind them. At that time all the activity which today takes place inside went on outdoors and was as noisy as an auction sale. I noticed a broker wildly gesticulating—probably a southerner, with his ruddy complexion and black hair, a shock of which fell across his forehead. Now smiling, now anguished, mopping his round face, he exhorted the crowd with sweeping gestures. That's my man, I thought. I aimed my camera and took a whole series of pictures.

I sent these photographs to various European magazines with the title, "Snapshots of the Paris Stock Exchange." Some time afterward I received clippings from a Belgian paper and discovered, to my great astonishment, my photos printed under a headline reading: RISE ON THE PARIS STOCK EXCHANGE. SHARES REACHING FABULOUS PRICES. Thanks to ingenious subtitles, my innocent little story was blown up to signify a financial event. My astonishment verged on stupefaction when a few days later I found the same photos in a German paper, this time under the heading: PANIC IN THE PARIS STOCK EXCHANGE. FORTUNES TOPPLE. THOUSANDS RUINED.

My pictures were a perfect illustration of the seller's despair and the speculator's bewilderment on the road to ruin. I began to perceive that the objectivity of a picture is merely an illusion. Descriptive captions can change the meaning entirely.

Under the heading "Information or Propaganda?" the

Paris Stock Exchange

weekly paper *L'Express,* in December 1956, published a double series of photos taken during the Hungarian rebellion—identical documents, but with their order changed and the commentary on them altered by the editor. The idea was to show how various government-run television stations could have used the same pictures to give absolutely contradictory but apparently truthful versions of the events.

A few examples:

Under a photo depicting a Russian tank in a street:

First caption: "In contempt of the people's right to self-determination, the Soviet government has sent armored divisions to Budapest to quell the uprising."

Second caption: "The Hungarian people have asked the Russian people for help. Russian tanks have been sent to protect the workers and to restore order."

Under a photo of Janos Kadar:

First caption: "Under the protection of Soviet tanks, the Stalinist Janos Kadar has formed a new government and established a reign of police terrorism."

Second caption: "But thanks to the drastic measures taken by the new government formed by Janos Kadar, unanimously supported by the populace, the rebellion has been put down."

Under a photograph depicting two young Hungarians:

First caption: "Despite the bloody repression by Soviet troops, Hungarian youth continues the struggle with shouts of 'Rather death than slavery.' "

Second caption: "Despite government appeals, fanatic counterrevolutionaries have refused to lay down their arms and have continued their hopeless struggle."

A change in the meaning of pictures may also result from the way they are juxtaposed, making it possible to suggest conclusions without resorting to captions.

In 1936 a new picture magazine appeared in the United States: *Life.* Its editor commissioned me to do a photo-story on the depressed areas in England, officially called "The Black Country." These highly industrialized areas had been centers of

the most prosperous industries during the last century, but were 35
very hard hit by the First World War and the Depression. Most
of the enterprises, established in the nineteenth century, used
old-fashioned methods and were no longer able to bear the
competition of modern factories. The owners found it more
profitable to abandon than to modernize them. They left the
region, but the population remained and became poverty
stricken. In 1936 there were almost two million unemployed in
England.

When I arrived at Newcastle-upon-Tyne, the entire city was
unemployed. The shipyards, with their buildings half falling to
pieces, resembled war-torn ruins. Between the tangled and rusty
rails grew rank weeds and a few wild flowers. I had the impression of visiting a cemetery. The unemployed lived on welfare
which was just enough to keep them and their families from
dying of hunger. I photographed wretched, debilitated men who
for years had been reduced to idleness. At Witton Park, in the
town of Bishop Aukland, my camera captured families of more
than eight people living together in only one room. The
women's faces were ravaged. They did not know how they would
pay the rent or feed their families. What would become of their
children? they kept asking me in despair.

During the same period the Simpson scandal broke out:
King Edward was in love with an American divorcée. All the
newspapers raged against him. English morality, still imbued
with Victorian rigor, could not accept Mrs. Simpson as queen.
The scandal was such that the king abdicated.

All of America was deeply offended by British public opinion. *Life* published my photographs under the innocuous heading: "This Is What Englishmen Mean by the Depressed Areas."
Right next to my pictures of poverty-stricken people they had
inserted a full-page photograph of Queen Mary, in a lace dress,
covered with jewels, a four-strand pearl choker round her neck,
holding one of her grandsons on her lap, and flanked by the two
princesses, entrancing in their immaculate dresses: Elizabeth
and Margaret Rose. The brutal contrast made any caption pointless: Mrs. Simpson was avenged in the eyes of liberal America.

Newcastle-upon-Tyne, England, 1936

LEFT: *Witton Park in the Bishop Aukland area, England, 1936*

Jarrow-upon-Tyne,
England, 1936

LEFT: *Maryport in*
Cumberland,
England, 1936

This is manipulation. But when photographs are deliberately employed to falsify facts, their use becomes an ethical problem.

In June 1966 the French magazine *Paris Match,* which at the time had a circulation of more than 1,200,000, published an eight-page story entitled: "Among the Nazis, '66."

Everyone was then expecting the party of the extreme right in Germany, the NPD (National Democratic Party), to win the elections scheduled to take place a month later in the provinces. Although twenty years had elapsed since the war, the French were still traumatized by the Nazi atrocities, and the existence

*Newcastle-upon-Tyne,
England, 1936*

of a party that regrouped all those who still yearned for the Third Reich appeared a terrifying prospect. The subject therefore bordered on big news, and the editors of the magazine considered it important enough to be announced on the cover.

The story began with a full page in color, depicting a boy, with a swastika armband on his white shirt, standing and raising his glass to three other young men. On the back wall was a huge Nazi flag. The caption read: "A party of Nazis in Bavaria bring out relics of the Reich, and as they drink their beer, again sing in chorus the 'Horst Wessel Lied.' "

The following pages showed a few pictures of the inhabitants of a Bavarian village and its mayor. The captions explained that these were former Nazis, although nothing in the photographs themselves would have led one to assume so. Then came a few photographs of the founder of the new party, and at the end, spread over two pages, in black and white, another "shock" picture—young men in SS uniforms, with the caption: "At the home of Peter Breuer, a native of Munich who owns a collection of four hundred SS and SA uniforms, a man nostalgic for the Third Reich salutes a bust of Hitler."

In England the *Daily Express* (with a circulation of over four million) reproduced the photograph of the young men raising their glasses; a few days later, in the Soviet Union, the picture, shown on television, reached an audience of a hundred million spectators.

Both photographs in the *Paris Match* article were fakes. One of the editors had obtained them by renting costumes from a dealer named Breuer. A few young Germans had agreed to pose for the reporter, convinced that it was for some practical joke. The group of men raising their glasses were the firemen of a small Bavarian village, for whom the editor of *Paris Match* had bought a barrel of beer, and who thought they were drinking to Franco-German friendship.

The German government protested in the German newspapers; innumerable articles denounced the fraud in detail; but millions of French, English, and Russian readers had seen the photographs and believed them to be genuine.

to come home late cry out despairingly: "Door, please!" and continue repeating that sacrosanct and hateful phrase until the concierge, finally awakened, was willing to work the door-pull or push the button over her head. Moreover, as you walked past her quarters, you had to call out your name before you could go up to your apartment.

At first, Madame Petit was very friendly to me, in spite of my blue wall.

She was short and fat. Her hair was held in place by combs decorated with fake pearls, and little curls covered her forehead and temples. Her husband, a worker at the Citroën plant, apparently earned a good living. She had two children. The whole family was crowded into her small quarters, consisting of one room and a kitchen. Never a ray of sun.

The French don't always care much about their homes; on the other hand, food counts a great deal. There is no doubt that the food of a concierge in France is better and more abundant

than that of an English duchess. I used to take my meals at a Russian restaurant on rue Lecourbe, not far from where I lived. The set price was 3.50 francs. I soon had my fill of borscht and blinis. Hearing my complaints, Madame Petit suggested taking me as a paying guest. I was delighted at the idea, but when she stated her price, I was dumbfounded: seven francs! When I confessed that I could not afford to pay that much, she cried out indignantly: "How can you expect me to charge any less? I spend almost that much for each of us! First of all, you've got to have appetizers—salami, ham, radishes, a hard-boiled egg, olives—then a vegetable; then you'll want a good steak, nice and tender, with french fries. You've also got to have a salad, then cheese and fruit; and finally, a good cup of coffee. And don't forget the wine!" Unable to accept the fact that her price was not within my budget, she shrugged her shoulders disdainfully and retired to her quarters.

Around that time several of my former classmates at the University of Frankfurt arrived in Paris, fleeing from Germany and persecution, like so many others. Despite the great influx of refugees, very few French people realized that Hitler's coming to power was a serious threat to peace in Europe.

Alix Guillain informed me that Madame Mayrisch de Saint-Hubert, along with her daughter Andrée and her husband, the deputy Pierre Viénot, had formed a committee to help the refugees. I was to draw their attention to cases worthy of interest. Many young students would come to me to talk about their problems. Some were hoping to continue their studies; others were looking for work. Among them was a young law student who, foreseeing the difficulties involved in going on with his studies, had learned photography. I suggested that he work with me. He was called Richard, and we invented a name for our business which was a combination of our first names: GIRIX (Gi, the first two letters of Gisèle, and Rix, the German nickname for Richard). Years later friends explained to me that the name did not sound right to French ears. Our knowledge of the French language was then still too rudimentary for us to have realized it. Rix rented a studio on the fourth floor of my building and we

Paris family

set up a darkroom in his kitchen. My studio was to be used for receiving prospective clients. I was able to devote only part of my time to photography, for I was still writing my thesis and taking courses at the Sorbonne. Rix soon built up quite a clientèle. He contributed to several small magazines and got orders for publicity photos. But orders for portraits were somewhat rare.

Other of my former classmates told me about the problems they were having putting themselves right with the authorities. I had the same experience myself when my passport expired. The employee at the German consulate looked stern. Instead of stamping my passport, she tore it up in rage:

"You are no longer a German citizen," she said curtly. My name was on the blacklist of undesirables who had manifestly refused Nazism. I recalled B. Traven's *Death Ship,* the story of a sailor who had lost his identification papers. His fellow sufferers are portrayed as pariahs doomed to the hardest and most humiliating work: the living dead, the "scum of the earth."

In 1941 Arthur Koestler was to publish a book under this title. He did not have his papers at that time either. The scum of the earth are those who are driven from their own countries.

7

*Small Causes,
Great Effects*

The winter of 1934–1935 was a hard one. I came down with pleurisy. As I was beginning to recuperate, the neighborhood doctor, who treated his patients mostly with cupping glasses and aspirin, advised me to go to the mountains. It was good advice. I was wondering how to finance my stay when I received a visit from Stanislas, one of my friends who worked in a photography shop near the Place Saint-Michel.

"I need a holiday too," he told me. "And I have a great idea. How about going to Megève?"

I knew how little he earned and was surprised at the suggestion.

"We're going to Megève not to spend money but to earn it; and we'll get a good rest," ' he declared confidently. "Haven't you seen the beach photographers at seaside places who offer to do portraits of the vacationers? Why couldn't we do the same thing in winter, on the ski slopes? The people who can't yet stand on their skis will be delighted to impress their families and friends!"

I found the idea ingenious. Lydia, Stanislas's girl friend, would come with us. She was a milliner. If she could not help us, she could at least do the cooking.

48   There were only half a dozen hotels and a very few shops
in Megève at the time. One of the shops attracted our attention,
for part of its window display consisted of postcards and photographic equipment. The owner, for a share in the profits, agreed
to exhibit our photographs as well.

I had my pockets filled with business cards. On one side
were the shop's trademark and address; on the other we had
printed:

> How funny you looked a few minutes ago!
> Wouldn't you like to admire yourself?
> Tomorrow you can . . .
> On a Girix photo . . .
> Try and see . . .

On the ski slopes I soon understood that in large part our
clients would be recruited from beginners. Those who were

Megève

attracted to the ground, as by a magnet, were the most en-
thusiastic: right on the slopes, of course, and in flawless position. The orders flooded in.

"Come tomorrow morning, a little before the lessons
start," begged one young woman, more notable for her elegance than her agility. "I'd like to be photographed with Lou-
lou." The next day she appeared with a tiny dog. A skier holding
a little Pekingese in her arms makes a somewhat curious picture,
but the client had to have her own way. Another, a rather ugly
and unobtrusive brunette, asked: "Would you please photograph me with the ski instructor?" He was a handsome, sunburned lad, with broad shoulders. She ordered twelve prints.
The photos were exhibited at five o'clock. We did not earn huge
amounts, but still enough to cover our expenses in Megève.

The weeks flew by. It was early in February. Every morning,
before proceeding to the ski classes, I would take the lift up to
Mont d'Arbois. It was the only time of the day I could ski for

Megève peasant woman

pleasure. But that happy hour of relaxation was to prove very costly. One beautiful sunny morning I bumped into a rock hidden under the snow, had a bad fall, and sprained my foot. And more serious, once back in my room I realized I had lost my Leica. We put an ad in the local paper offering a reward to anyone who would restore my precious tool, but the camera was not to be found and we had to return to Paris.

8

I Become a Spy

The first thing I noted on my return was that Rix had disappeared. His apartment was in order and looked as if he had left it just five minutes before. All his things were there in their proper places. The concierge claimed to know nothing about it. I telephoned some mutual friends. No one had seen him. His empty suitcases were stacked above the wardrobe; none were missing. Rix was an orderly boy. He was not the type to disappear without at least leaving a message. Two days later, just as I was about to notify the police, I received a letter from him, mailed in Amsterdam:

"Last Thursday, at seven in the morning, two police inspectors came to my place and gave me notice that I was to be deported. They didn't give me time to pack my suitcases, but took me straight from my apartment to the station, got into the train with me, and did not leave me until we reached the Belgian border! I was unable to get any explanation at all out of them. Do what you can to clarify the situation. There must have been some frightful misunderstanding. I don't understand why the French authorities, who had allowed me to enter the country without any problem, have deported me so suddenly and in such a brutal way."

51

—he had contacted my concierge and, to get his information, had impressed her with the gravity of the inquiry.

A private detective! All at once the truth began to dawn on me. It was he who had aroused my concierge's suspicion—she who read nothing but newspaper detective stories!

"Madame Petit, tell me: the man who came to see you to get information concerning me, what did he talk to you about?"

"Oh, leave me alone. I didn't say anything. It's not my fault if the police are looking for you!" This time she lost her temper. "To think that we have to lodge people like you," she shouted. "You, with your death's-heads on the wall!"

"But Madame, those are enlargements of coffee beans!"

"Leave me alone, I know the Swiss police are after you: you wanted to photograph maneuvers, and when they caught you at it, you threw your camera away."

Now I myself became enraged.

"You made up that whole story or else you didn't understand it properly; I lost my camera when I fell coming down a ski run. It's you who notified the police, saying that you had an idea they were looking for me in Switzerland!"

I slowly climbed back up the stairs. Rix had been accused of taking photographs of nudes, no doubt because the concierge had denounced him. And now she had decided I was a spy.

I later learned that Madame Petit's father had been killed by a German shell during the Great War and that she profoundly hated everyone who lived across the Rhine! Merely being born in Germany was enough to make one a criminal in her eyes.

9

*Two
Paris Bookshops
and a Recipe*

One chilly morning in March I was walking down the rue de
l'Odéon, looking in the shop windows. A cat was sleeping in a
Louis XV armchair in an antique shop. Next door the owner of
a dairy store, wearing a white smock, was putting away boxes of
cheese. Farther on I noticed a small bookshop painted entirely
gray. Over the door, in large letters, was a sign reading: 'La
Maison des Amis des Livres. Lending Library. Bookshop. A.
Monnier.''

Standing in front of the window was a box filled with books
for sale. I stopped to look through it and discovered a small
volume by Jules Romains entitled *Puissances de Paris.* It had been
published in 1919 by the *Nouvelle Revue Française.* Everything
relating to Paris fascinated me. The price was very reasonable,
so I walked in, and there in front of me, sitting at a large table,
I saw a very round little woman, barely forty, filing index cards.
She had a very high forehead, and her straight brown hair was
cut short. Over a woolen sweater, with a small round collar, she
was wearing a gray vest, and the pleats of her long skirt, cut from
the same cloth, touched the ground. It was Adrienne Monnier,
the owner. She raised her head and looked at me with an en-

couraging smile. Her brown-green eyes reflected a sharp and somewhat mischievous mind. Her small features were delicately chiseled, and her pink complexion was astonishingly fresh. Her whole person exuded serenity.

It was warm in the shop, thanks to a gently simmering coal stove. The walls disappeared behind shelves of books covered in transparent paper. At a long table several customers were leafing through the latest books and periodicals. The walls were covered with portraits of writers.

I walked up shyly, holding out the small book I wished to purchase. Adrienne Monnier began a conversation straightaway. It was not long before she knew that I was a student and

had fled Nazism. In a very clear and curiously high voice, she inquired about my literary tastes and encouraged me to take out a subscription to her lending library, promising to guide me through contemporary French literature.

I soon realized that Adrienne was famous in literary circles. Almost all the well-known writers, as well as those just beginning, frequented her bookshop. It was there that Paul Valéry spoke in public for the first time, that André Gide read from his *Fruits of the Earth*, that Jules Romains recited his *Europe* in 1917, that Léon-Paul Fargue read his poems. Apollinaire, Paul Claudel, Valéry Larbaud, James Joyce, T. S. Eliot, André Breton, Louis Aragon, Paul Eluard: the long list of those who had made

Adrienne Monnier, 1935

the shop their gathering place was an impressive tribute to the woman who presided over it. I became a regular visitor on the rue de l'Odéon, where I met many of my future models.

On my first visit to Adrienne's, she suggested taking me across the street to introduce me to her friend Sylvia Beach, who had an American bookshop almost directly opposite. Shakespeare and Company had been founded in 1920 and was as famous as the Maison des Amis des Livres.

Sylvia Beach, born in Baltimore, was descended from generations of clergymen. She had grown up in Princeton, New Jersey, where her father, the Reverend Sylvester Woodbridge Beach, D.D., had been pastor of the First Presbyterian Church for seventeen years. She had made literary history in 1922 as the publisher of James Joyce's *Ulysses*, which no professional publisher would accept for fear of being prosecuted. Considered obscene at the time, *Ulysses* had been banned both in America and in England. In publishing it, the clergyman's daughter had shown extraordinary perception and great courage.

In contrast to Adrienne, Sylvia was tall and slim. She was always modestly dressed in tweed suits. With her short hair, warm complexion, and ever-smiling eyes, she still appeared youthful, though approaching her fifties. She received me, just a young student at the time, as kindly and simply as she did the great writers who frequented her shop. What struck me most was her way of seeing people and things with a kind of dry humor that was typically American.

During one of my first visits she showed me two original drawings by William Blake and a page of a Walt Whitman manuscript. Both were artists she deeply admired. The walls of Shakespeare and Company were covered with photographs of now-famous writers: James Joyce, of course, with a black patch over one eye, Ezra Pound, Ernest Hemingway, Sinclair Lewis, Katherine Anne Porter, Scott Fitzgerald, and many others. But by the time I met her, in 1935, she was having serious financial problems. Her venture as publisher of *Ulysses* had been ruinous. During the typesetting of his huge book, Joyce began to make countless corrections in proof. She let him do what he wanted,

Sylvia Beach at Shakespeare and Company, 1937

and it is thanks to her indulgence that Joyce was able to polish his very original style in all its detail. But the costs of printing rose sharply. Then, in the late twenties, with America hit by the Depression, the American writers who had made her bookshop their mailbox, those whom Gertrude Stein called "the Lost Generation" (very wrongly, according to Sylvia Beach), had been forced to return home. The crowds of American tourists stopped pouring in for the same reason. Among French readers there were many enthusiasts of Anglo-American literature, but such customers were not enough to support Shakespeare and Company. Since the English-language books were always bound, they sold for much higher prices than the French paperbacks and found few buyers.

It was André Gide, Sylvia's great friend, who—learning that she might have to close—was the first of the writers to be upset. Gide, Paul Valéry, Léon-Paul Fargue, Jean Paulhan, and a few others formed a committee called the Friends of Shakespeare and Company. The members paid annual dues, which entitled them to attend readings of unpublished works, read by the authors themselves. I had the privilege, starting in January 1936, of attending readings given by Gide, Valéry, Jean Schlumberger, Paulhan, T. S. Eliot, and others. It was then that I met Ernest Hemingway. Hundreds of times since, I have been reproached for not having taken advantage of the opportunity to photograph him. I was probably too shy and too impressed by his thundering voice.

Hemingway had a horror of speaking in public. He had agreed to do so out of friendship for Sylvia, and on condition that Stephen Spender would speak at the same time and that plenty of beer be available. "It will flow," Sylvia promised him with a broad smile as we dined together at Adrienne's the night before the performance. Hemingway read a few passages from his yet unpublished novel *To Have and Have Not*, and Stephen Spender recited some poems on the Spanish civil war, from which he had just returned. The audience, among whom were James Joyce and Paul Valéry, was so large that the heat became stifling. Stephen Spender seemed completely at ease, while

Hemingway kept mopping his brow and looking at the audience like a bull confronting a toreador. Empty beer cans piled up on the table.

I was less intimidated by Thornton Wilder. He was then professor of comparative literature at the University of Chicago and was accustomed to young people. Since he liked the portraits I did of him, he invited me to dinner with Adrienne. He took us to a little restaurant behind the Halles au Vin, a market which no longer exists. The restaurant was not much to look at, and the floor was covered with sawdust. Wilder ordered lobster à l'Américaine from the owner. I had never eaten it before. A huge quantity was served, and the three of us just barely managed to finish it. It was so delicious that I dreamed of having an opportunity to eat it again. On my first visit to New York, in 1948, I asked friends of mine to take me to a good seafood restaurant. We went to the King of the Sea. I ordered a "lobster, American style," from the waiter and was rejoicing at the thought of the delectable feast I would soon be devouring. The waiter looked at me, uncomprehending. "Lobster American style? Never heard of it." I was extremely disappointed when he brought me the usual American dish of broiled lobster. It was not until I returned to France that I learned that "lobster à l'Américaine" (which some say is a distortion of à l'Armoricaine) is a specialty of Brittany.

The dish is so fine that I cannot resist the temptation to give a recipe for it here: Cut live lobsters into pieces and throw them into a large skillet containing sizzling butter and oil. Stew until the shells turn red. Add a tablespoon of chopped shallots, parsley, and tarragon, then a minute later, a touch of crushed garlic. Sprinkle with $1/5$ cup of brandy and touch with a lighted match. When the flame has gone out, pour in a half bottle of white wine and some tomato purée. Cook for twenty minutes. Every good French cookbook has the recipe, but I hope that these brief directions will make my readers' mouths water.

10

André Malraux

One day in April 1935 I received a note from André Malraux. *Man's Fate*, for which he had been awarded the Prix Goncourt the year before, was to be reprinted and he needed photographs. I asked him to come to my place. At the appointed time he appeared, dressed in an old raincoat which, to look his usual self, he wanted to wear while posing.

I felt uncomfortable. I had photographed unknown faces and my friends, but this portrait was my first important commission. Here before me stood one of the great writers of the time, and my photograph was to make his face familiar to the entire world.

Malraux walked onto the terrace. His slim form stood out against the pale gray Paris sky; he was leaning forward slightly, smoking his cigarette. Once again I was struck by the silky quality of his hair, his anxious eyes, his almost feminine lips. His restless eyes would wander from one point to another. If only —I thought, watching him through my viewer—if only I could catch him in action and immobilize one of his gestures, it would express the man far better than any mere picture of his face.

"Malraux, do you think photography is an art?"

André Malraux, 1935

"Photography may be an art, or it may simply be a desire to record images," he responded.

Then he gave me a whole lecture on photography as a means of reproducing works of art. Through photography, paintings had entered every home; it had democratized art. But at the same time, through the change of scale, it had falsified it. One inordinately enlarged detail could give a very false idea of the original.

He spoke with incredible volubility and intensity; each new idea collided with the previous one. He gave me a preview of his *Museum Without Walls*. Absorbed by the task at hand, I hardly managed to follow him. I was observing him through the lens, ready to release the shutter. I felt frustrated; I would have preferred to listen. But I had managed to divert his attention from the camera and thus was able to get a natural picture of him. Afterward, again and again, I found myself in the position of facing a creative person and of being obliged to pay but little attention to what he was saying. In time I managed to develop a technique for leading my model to talk about things that concerned him, with only one purpose in mind: to make him forget the camera.

It was windy outside, and with one hand Malraux was nervously pushing his silky hair back from his face, unaware that I had pressed the button several times while he was talking. Soon I had finished.

"Already?" he asked with surprise.

Overcome by weariness from such concentrated effort, I assured him I was finished. Was he going to like my pictures? One of them fortunately pleased him: it was to travel around the world.

Three years later, in 1938, I had the opportunity to photograph him again. He was leaving for Spain, slimmer than ever, more haunted, more nervous, as if driven by some hidden goal. He was then a militant member of the extreme left.

Shortly after the Liberation of France in 1945 we met again. Under De Gaulle's first government he had become Minister of Information. He was thus able to help me bring to France several tons of food and clothing I had collected in South America. They were destined for the French intellectuals, still living under great material difficulties.

Long afterwards, in 1952, he asked me to photograph certain *objets d'art* for his *Museum Without Walls*. Now and again we met at official openings of exhibitions or at political meetings of the Gaullist party, but we had exchanged little more than smiles. During all these years I had been traveling extensively abroad and was not often in France. Therefore it wasn't until June 1967 that we had a long private talk again. By then Malraux was Minister of Cultural Affairs, and I was assailed by newspapers and magazines asking me to photograph him for the publication of his *Anti-Memoirs* which were due to come out shortly. *Paris-Match* was to publish extracts from this book and wanted a color photograph of the author for its cover.

I had photographed Malraux several times in his office, but now I suggested that I take some pictures at his home, feeling that they would be more intimate and he more relaxed. Malraux agreed and asked me to come to the estate near Versailles, on the road to Saint-Cyr, where he had been living ever since the OAS had thrown a bomb into his Boulogne apartment. The driver of the taxi I took from the station was talkative. I was not, he told me, the first person he had taken to the Minister's.

"He's lucky to live in such a beautiful house; not just anybody can have a place like that!"

He was probably unaware that Malraux's residence belonged to the state. The taxi entered a private drive, at the end of which stood a one-story building, half château, half country house, surrounded by a park.

I perceived the tall figure of Malraux on the steps.

"I can give you only an hour," he said. We walked through a series of rooms, filled with period furniture and works of art.

"They're not mine," said Malraux, as if apologizing.

But the choices had been his and clearly showed his preferences. I noticed a huge Dufy tapestry representing Paris, and several paintings by Dubuffet.

"Do excuse me," I said, preoccupied, for the minutes were

slipping by, "I came to photograph you, not your house."

"Well, then, let's go outside!"

The park, with its statues, was admirable: a miniature park of Versailles. A white kitten ran after the writer.

"It's the issue of a Siamese that sinned with an alley cat," said Malraux, lifting it up. When he stretched out his arm, the cat ran along it. I snapped a picture. It was the photograph that *Match* was to select for its cover.

General de Gaulle, with André Malraux, 1967

André Malraux, 1935

Malraux kept walking up and down, trying to smile and to be natural, but he remained terribly stiff, far too aware of being photographed. In order to relieve his tension I tried, once again, the old trick of directing our conversation toward subjects that I knew particularly interested him. We spoke about the cleaning of the buildings of Paris, which had been his idea. Thanks to him, over a thousand years of dirt had disappeared from the city's monuments and given it a fresh, exciting appearance. He told me about his effort to bring art nearer to the people by establishing "Maisons de la Culture" throughout the country. He mentioned his plans to modernize the museums and the difficulty of changing old administrative routines. All his plans were motivated by his profound patriotism. Suddenly I understood his fascination for General de Gaulle, and why these two great men, with such different backgrounds and experiences, felt such a mutual attraction: they shared a belief in the greatness of France. He told me he had seen many of my photographs and that he thought very highly of my work. I observed him through my lens. How he had changed! He had aged, his features had become thicker, but what struck me above all was the expression in his eyes, full of sadness and anxiety. It was over thirty years ago that I had taken the photo on my terrace—a whole lifetime; and his had been filled with tragedy.

During the war his wife had died. His only brother had been killed by the Gestapo. Just a short while before my visit, his two adolescent sons had been killed in an automobile accident. He had suffered profoundly; now he had reached the height of fame. That sense of adventure which had taken him to Asia and Spain, and drawn him into the Resistance, had finally brought him to serve the state. But death, which had always haunted him and had been at the core of his art as a novelist, had struck at his personal life. Suddenly, behind the façade of the statesman, I caught a glimpse of the human being, whose eyes expressed —probably without his realizing it—profound despair.

André Malraux, 1967

11

Congress for the Freedom of Culture

There are years that leave absolutely no trace in our minds, like dreams we forget on waking. Others we remember all our lives. The people I met and the friendships I made in 1935 had a profound influence on my destiny: it is a year I have never forgotten.

In Germany the law protecting pure blood officially sanctioned racial persecution, and the swastika was declared the nation's flag. In France the leftist parties combined to form the Popular Front. Russia became the scene of the purge trials of the Stalinist era. Italy invaded Abyssinia.

The most important books of the year were Sinclair Lewis's *It Can't Happen Here*, Thornton Wilder's *Heaven's My Destination*, and Thomas Wolfe's *Of Time and the River*. George Gershwin's opera *Porgy and Bess* was performed for the first time in New York. In Paris, Louis Jouvet directed Jean Giraudoux's *Tiger at the Gates*. Greta Garbo starred in *Anna Karenina*.

In the United States the CIO was founded; the Gallup Institute began its studies of public opinion. Everyone was dancing the rumba. The price of permanent waves had gone down: a new hair style, the pageboy, was all the rage.

Materially, my life was not easy, but I was young and optimistic. I had now been settled in Paris for two years. Since the German consulate had refused to renew my passport, I was stateless. I had finished my thesis on the history of photography, but until I had the means to have it printed, as the Sorbonne required, I could not defend it. I was beginning to earn a little money by doing photo-stories, in collaboration with a young writer, a surrealist, René Crevel, who supplied the texts; our joint effort ended tragically. Crevel committed suicide in June. I learned of his death at a meeting at the Maison de la Mutualité, where I was attending a Congress for the Freedom of Culture. It was rare to see so many brilliant men of letters, from thirty-five countries, gathered together. Their ideas on philosophy, literature, and politics differed, but they were all united in a common desire to defend freedom of the mind from Fascism and the impending war. The French delegation was the largest. The Congress had been organized by André Malraux, whose eloquence and fiery spirit fascinated the audience.

"The new humanism we wish to create, and which has its roots in an intellectual tradition from Voltaire to Marx, demands, above all, that man be fully aware of his true reality. Being a man means reducing one's illusions and bad faith to a minimum," he declared. At that time he believed that "communism restores creativity to the individual."

The most famous Frenchman present was André Gide. He, too, had lately been won over to the cause of the working classes.

"I claim that I can be profoundly international and yet remain profoundly French. Just as I claim that I have remained profoundly individualistic, despite my full approbation of communism and, indeed, with the help of communism. For my thesis has always been this: that the more each person is himself, the better he will serve the community. Today this thesis is complemented by another, its counterpart or corollary: that each individual, and the personal characteristics of each individual, may flourish most perfectly in a communistic society."

After his trip to the U.S.S.R., André Gide was to change his mind altogether, just as André Malraux was to do a few years later.

I also remember Henri Barbusse, whose face was already consumed by tuberculosis; Aldous Huxley, who, behind his thick glasses, was half blind; Bertolt Brecht, with his shy smile and his head shaved like a prisoner's; Ilya Ehrenburg, with his lion's mane; Heinrich Mann, who looked like a peaceful bourgeois; the Dane, Martin Andersen Nexø; Boris Pasternak, who was then still unknown, for his poems had not yet been translated. At the Congress he said about poetry: "It will always be an undergrowth; one will always have to bend down to perceive it; it will always be too simple to be discussed at meetings. Poetry will remain forever the organic function of a happy creature, overflowing with the full joy of language; will ever be found clenched within a native heart bursting with its burden: the greater mankind's happiness, the easier it will be to be an artist."

The photograph I took of Pasternak at the time shows him young and smiling, like his words. Unlike Gide, he was not concerned about finding a justification for his individualism. He flourished not because of communist society, nor in opposition to it, but by virtue of a purely natural impulse. His only universe was poetry.

If a congress of that importance were to be held today, a hundred photographers would rush there to take pictures; in 1935 only I was there, with Chim, who a few years later, when he became a naturalized United States citizen, was to be known as David Seymour. Although the hall was dark, I did not want to use flashes, for magnesium, used then, made an irritating noise. Since film was not as sensitive as it is today, a number of my photos were underexposed. They looked like "solarizations." The effect is surprising, for the picture becomes a pattern.

OPPOSITE: *André Malraux. Congress for the Freedom of Culture, 1935*
ABOVE: *Julien Benda, André Gide, André Malraux. Congress for the Freedom of Culture, 1935* RIGHT: *André Gide, Congress for the Freedom of Culture, 1935*

Ilya Ehrenburg, André Malraux, Paul Nizan. Congress for the Freedom of Culture, 1935

Aldous Huxley.
Congress for the
Freedom of Culture,
1935

Henri Barbusse, 1935

Boris Pasternak. Congress for the Freedom of Culture, 1935

12

Photography:
A Dangerous
Profession

The fact of having attended the writers' congress, even in the capacity of a mere photographer, must have lengthened my file at Police Headquarters. I received a deportation order, but in contrast to Rix, I was generously allowed forty-eight hours to pack my bags. However, I no longer had a passport, and no country in the world would have admitted me.

I went to Adrienne Monnier for advice. She had displayed a great deal of concern for me and had invited me to her home several times. Adrienne's hospitality to me was exceptional: French families have always been difficult about accepting foreigners. This was even truer before the war, when the French traveled less than they do today. Everything foreign was looked upon with some suspicion. At the time, I associated mostly with other German refugees—not so much because we spoke the same language, as because we shared a similar fate. Most of my friends had no contact with Parisians. If the French seem less hospitable than Americans, for example, the reason lies in their different conception of hospitality. When the French invite guests, they want to entertain in style, and that implies a great amount of preparation. Americans, on the other hand, readily invite foreigners and offer them anything that happens to be in the refrigerator.

Adrienne Monnier's warm welcome gave me the courage to go to see her. I told her my whole story. I was to be deported, but was unable to go, since, without a passport, no country would admit me. If I did not leave France, I would be jailed. Adrienne was completely astonished. Like most people, she considered the police a necessary social evil, but one it was better not to meddle with. She clasped her hands as if in prayer, a gesture she often made while reflecting, and suggested that I move in with her until the whole affair was clarified. The fact of living in a French home would protect me.

"After all, the police wouldn't dare come to my place!" The statement showed her naïveté. I accepted her offer gratefully and moved in that day.

The next day I called at the deportation bureau at Police Headquarters. The waiting room was packed. Policemen were more or less gruffly trying to direct the flood of people to the proper channels. The air was filled with the smell of perspiration and tobacco. The whole crowd of foreigners—men and women, many of whom had their children with them—was anxious and frightened. Numbers were distributed, indicating the order in which each would be taken. I had arrived at eight in the morning and had to wait until three in the afternoon. The employee, behind his window, seemed as prostrate as I myself. I explained that I had no passport. He listened without making any comment and granted me a week's reprieve. When I asked why I was being deported, he had no answer; it was none of his business. *"Débrouillez-vous!"* he advised me; in other words, "You'll have to cope and find a way out for yourself."

"Débrouillez-vous!" That very French and all but untranslatable little phrase was still ringing in my ears when I got back to the rue de l'Odéon. Adrienne gave me the idea of speaking to my Sorbonne professors; their testimony on my behalf would be above suspicion. I went to see the philosopher Léon Brunschvicg. He greeted me kindly and gave me a letter of recommendation. Célestin Bouglé, my economics professor, also agreed to

write me one, as did Charles Lalo, who had accepted my thesis. The most heartwarming testimony came from the abbey of Pontigny. Paul Desjardins had founded the "Décades de l'abbaye de Pontigny," ten-day gatherings at which writers, philosophers, professors, and students of all countries could meet and exchange ideas. There one might encounter André Gide, Roger Martin du Gard, François Mauriac, Charles du Bos, André Malraux, or Jean-Paul Sartre, as well as Englishmen such as Lytton Strachey, Germans such as Bernard Groethuysen, Ernst Robert Curtius or Walter Benjamin, and Russians like Berdyaev and Alexander Koyré. In addition to the "Décades," Paul Desjardins had created at Pontigny a center for study and relaxation.

L'Abbaye de Pontigny

Originally Cistercian, the abbey is situated in the Yonne,
amid peaceful meadows crisscrossed by small rivers and rows of
poplar trees. A large garden with hedgerows surrounded the
house, which stood next to the church. The library contained
20,000 volumes.

I had gone to Pontigny for the first time in the summer of
1934. Paul Desjardins, who was then over seventy, was waiting
for me at the little Saint-Florentin station. Tall, though somewhat bent with age, he was wearing a large velvet beret.

We took our meals in what was formerly the monks' refec-
tory. During my first stay there, when my future looked very
bleak, the peace of the old stones and Paul Desjardins' kindness

Paul Desjardins, 1938

had been a great comfort. When Desjardins learned of my financial difficulties, he suggested that I photograph the abbey from every aspect and sell the photos to his guests. I thus, from time to time, would receive small money orders, each with a handwritten and detailed statement of accounts. In the letter he now sent me, intended for the French authorities, he suggested that he adopt me, if it would serve as a guarantee.

In order to add letters of recommendation from writers to all those I already had, Adrienne Monnier paid a visit to the *Nouvelle Revue Française.* She returned extremely upset: the meeting had taken place in Jean Paulhan's office, in the presence of his wife Germaine and a few writers. Jean Paulhan had commented: "Gisèle Freund deported? That doesn't surprise me. Everyone knows she sells photos of nudes under the tables at the Dôme."

"Jean, how can you say such a thing?" his wife exclaimed. "You just made that story up out of your head."

Paulhan nevertheless contributed a letter of recommendation in his beautiful handwriting: he was an admirable calligrapher.

"If she hasn't a passport anymore," one writer had said, "maybe she's a spy who's done for now!"—to the imaginative mind of a novelist, the simplest explanation.

Adrienne had then gone to see Madame Charlety, wife of the rector of the Sorbonne and one of her friends and subscribers.

"One never knows where the truth lies," she told Adrienne, advising her not to get mixed up in such a shady business.

"Tell me," Adrienne asked, visibly shaken, "did you really photograph nothing that was forbidden?"

I was speechless. No answer was possible. I felt I was forsaken by everybody and that I alone knew I had nothing with which to reproach myself.

Immediately Adrienne pulled herself together.

"I believe you," she said. "I'll do everything I can to help."

When I look back today at the situation, it appears laughable, but at the time I saw it differently. I was then a very young girl, separated from my family and living alone in a foreign country, struggling to support myself. Later millions of refugees had a far more tragic fate, but we were the avant-garde, the first to come to France since the Russian Revolution. Thousands of German refugees had flooded in; many had crossed the border illegally. They had been generously admitted, but in complete anarchy. Now the government, suddenly faced with them as a material problem—most of the refugees had no money—tried to get rid of them as quickly as possible, and under any pretext, beginning with the most suspicious cases. And a photographer was by definition a dangerous character.

I submitted all my letters of recommendation to Police Headquarters and soon received a summons. Adrienne decided to go along with me. An orderly took us through innumerable corridors, led us into an underground passage, and finally had us climb up several flights of stairs.

"Where are you taking us?" Adrienne asked in surprise.

"To the intelligence bureau of counterespionage," he answered indifferently.

"It's really too much, my having to go to such a place," muttered Adrienne.

We were led into a room that looked out onto the quay. An elegantly dressed young man was sitting behind a desk. I learned subsequently that he was private secretary to the head of the Security Section. He had been put in charge of my case. The police were probably intrigued by the number and fame of those vouching for me.

Through the open window I saw a barge gliding down the Seine. On the deck a woman was hanging out her laundry. If only I could have been in her place! I felt defenseless before this huge administrative machine which had singled me out and was now giving me such importance.

When the young man discovered who had come with me, he jumped up and offered us chairs.

"I've contributed to the *Mouton Blanc*," he said. It was a small literary review that Jules Romains had edited. "Unfortunately, I no longer have any time for literature.

"Your case is shocking; I've rarely seen such a bad file!"

He began to ask me lots of questions. My answers did not satisfy him. Suddenly he began to attack.

"After all, you've already had dealings with the police!"

"Me? Never!"

Then, in a flash, I remembered.

I had visited Paris for the first time in 1931. The trip had been a present from my father after I had passed my college entrance exams. One morning, as I was coming up out of the métro at Concorde, a police officer ordered me to climb into a Black Maria. The wagon was full. At the police station, when they examined identification papers, I realized that I did not have my passport with me. Everybody was released but me. I was not allowed to telephone the German consulate, and at nightfall I was locked into a cell, directly opposite a urinal. At that time I knew hardly any French. I had eaten nothing since morning. Finally, a young Alsatian policeman, who understood German, brought me a sandwich. Luckily, I at least had some money with me. No sooner had I stretched out on a kind of filthy mattress than a policeman entered my cell and sat next to me. His intentions were obvious, and I had great difficulty getting rid of him. From time to time men would come and urinate opposite my cell making obscene remarks. I did not close my eyes the whole night. At dawn I was taken to Headquarters. A dark room, blinding floodlights, questions. I did not understand half of what they were saying to me. In the end one of the policemen said:

"If you sign this statement, we'll release you immediately."

I was afraid and could think of only one thing: leaving, leaving at any price. I still, today, have no idea what I signed!

I proceeded directly to the German consulate, where I was told that I had been picked up in a raid, for the method common to police all over the world is to arrest everyone who happens to be on the scene of a demonstration.

"What demonstration?"

The consul shrugged his shoulders. "Probably a demonstration of the extreme left. In the future don't ever again go about without your identification papers."

So it was *that* which, four years later, was being thrown at me as a criminal past! I had never been involved in politics in France. As a foreigner, I refrained from taking part in any demonstrations. On the other hand, some of my friends were politically committed, and I never hid the fact that I was against Fascism, which I had fought in Germany. Could giving my opinion be considered a violation? I tried to defend myself. It was clear that the official did not believe me.

I have now forgotten how many times he had me return to his office. He had granted an extension of my stay. Adrienne Monnier's presence surely had something to do with it. Every time I left Police Headquarters, I felt more discouraged, as if I had been fighting windmills. I could no longer concentrate on my work. My brother, who was a refugee in London, came to spend a few days in Paris. When I tried to explain to him that I was accused not only of espionage but of communist activities, he burst out laughing. He simply could not take my story seriously.

Finally, Monsieur D. announced to me that he no longer believed I was guilty. He even read me certain passages from my file, every sentence of which began: "It would appear . . ." There were still a few more weeks of uncertainty. Then the police dropped the case, since they were unable to furnish the slightest proof to substantiate the charges brought against me. As Monsieur D. admitted to me: "Policemen are urged to make a show of their zeal. Sometimes they go too far. I've seen worse."

Those words did not console me. I had lost a lot of time and was still traumatized. My case was closed, but I was informed that it would remain in the files. From then on, I was officially on record as suspicious, thanks to a raid, a somewhat dishonest Swiss, and a concierge.

When the German troops occupied France, that same Monsieur D. became a high official in Vichy. He procured me a visa so that I might flee yet again. During the Liberation he asked me to testify on his behalf: he was being prosecuted for having collaborated. A curious reversal of situations.

That innocuous police matter was to have serious consequences, for my file did in fact fall into the hands of the Gestapo. As for me, I was no longer the same person. From that time on, I was ashamed of being a German. When I was made a French citizen and received a new passport, I wanted to go so far as to change my name, just to forget my past. My French friends no longer understood me.

"There are so many Parisians who were born in other countries," said Adrienne Monnier. "What difference does it make if they come from Paris or Warsaw or New York or Berlin? All that counts is intelligence and talent. France's greatness lies in the tolerant spirit in which she has always received foreigners." But the experience I had just had made me insensitive to such arguments: a spring had broken inside me. Every time I encountered a police officer in the street, I crossed to the other side.

One day, having found a birth certificate that gave my birthplace as Schöneberg, I insisted that it be substituted for Berlin on my passport, just as a New Yorker from Manhattan might have Brooklyn inscribed in his passport, or a Parisian, Auteuil. I also begged the authorities not to mention that Schöneberg was in Germany; I had learned that there was a small Alsatian village by the same name.

Because of the Nazi atrocities, people everywhere looked upon Germans with horror. They did not always make the distinction between the victims of the regime and its partisans. It would have taken a psychiatrist to understand me.

13

French Women Have No Rights

André Malraux tried to persuade Gaston Gallimard to publish my thesis at the *NRF,* but his efforts came to nothing. It was Adrienne Monnier who then suggested that she take it for her small publishing house. I was delighted; she had published an excellent literary review, *Le Navire d'Argent,* as well as books by writers like Paul Valéry and the famous French translation of James Joyce's *Ulysses.* Not only did Adrienne think highly of my study, but she was always ready to support the cause of women.

In *The Second Sex* Simone de Beauvoir described the state of dependency of French women until World War II. Legally, they had no rights. I myself had some experience of this when I married. I was not able to open a bank account, apply for a passport, or make the slightest business transaction without my husband's permission. In the world of letters a woman was relegated to the background. She was just about good enough to help her husband in his career, act as his secretary, and type his manuscripts; she was expected, above all, not to show too much spirit. With very rare exceptions, such as Colette, no woman in France was considered a great writer. At the Maison des Amis des Livres, Adrienne had published a small volume of short stories signed "J. M. Sollier," which, when it came out in 1932, was greatly admired in her literary circle. Everyone wanted to meet the author, but Adrienne explained that the young man preferred to remain incognito. Finally, Léon-Paul Fargue let the cat out of the bag: hiding behind the pseudonym "J. M. Sollier" was Adrienne Monnier herself. All praise came to an end. Not one of the writers would accept the fact that Adrienne could have a talent for writing or be anything other than a bookseller, for as a bookseller she was useful to them. She was still somewhat bitter about it, and every time she could help a woman to gain recognition, she did so fervently. Besides, she liked Germany for having contributed a number of geniuses to European civilization—Bach, Goethe, Kant, Hegel, Beethoven, Hölderlin —and she liked the Germans, "a worthy, good-natured people, wonderfully devoted to their work." But the violence and anti-Semitism of the Nazi regime filled her with horror, as one can see in her *Gazette.* For her I was a victim of Fascism, and there was no doubt I could count on her as a friend.

I defended my thesis at the Sorbonne in 1936. I had completed my studies at the university, and there was nothing now to prevent me from devoting myself entirely to photography.

14

The Eye of the Camera

I never again went anywhere without my camera. It had become
my third eye.

By almost imperceptibly shifting our eyes, we are able to see
a whole group of things simultaneously. In one glance we take
in not only the street but the houses, the sky, the passersby, and
the gestures they make. There is the milkman, setting two bottles in front of the door across the street; next to me is the
postman, in his blue uniform, delivering letters to my concierge.
I catch the curious look in her eyes as she makes out the various
names and addresses; but that is not enough: she turns the
envelopes over to find out who sent them. Up the street a beggar
is asking for charity. He is blind, but only during the day, for I
remember having seen him reading the newspapers one evening
in a neighborhood café. The door of the corner bakery opens
and out walks a housewife with two long loaves of bread under
one arm and a net bag filled with food in her hand. It is almost
noon; lunchtime is approaching. A truck loaded with furniture
moves slowly down the middle of the street. True: it is September 30, and the second-floor tenants are moving.

While the human eye absorbs innumerable details, the camera eye selects: therein lies its power, if one knows how to use it. Aimed at the milkman across the street, it never wanders toward the postman or the concierge; the camera must choose between the beggar and the housewife, the vault of the sky and the pavement; it captures an isolated reality in a fraction of a second. The immediate present thus takes on a symbolic value, which—if the photograph has meaning—awakens in the observer an endless series of associations of ideas and emotions.

A photograph cannot go beyond what the photographer intended. *I* am the one who decides at exactly what moment the button must be pressed. *I* choose the precise angle from which a scene will be taken. Twenty photographers standing right where I am when I focus will see different images. Each individual, with his particular sensitivity, perceives the same subject in his own unique way. And in the end, the intrinsic value of the photograph depends on the photographer's ability to select, among a mass of impressive and jumbled details, those that will reveal the most meaning.

Technical knowledge is of small account; above all, one must learn to *see.*

"I name that man an artist who *creates* forms . . . and I call that man an artisan who *reproduces* forms, however great may be the charm or sophistication of his craftsmanship," said André Malraux in his *Voices of Silence.* A photographer can master all the tricks of his trade and produce a technically perfect photograph; if his picture is interchangeable with anyone else's, no matter how good a technician he is, he is merely an artisan.

I had wanted to be a sociologist because the extreme diversity of social problems fascinated me. I became a photographer out of necessity, but I have never regretted it, for I soon understood that my most vital concerns were directed toward the individual, with his sorrows and hopes and anguishes. My camera led me to pay special heed to that which I took most to heart: a gesture, a sign, an isolated expression. Gradually, I came to believe that everything was summed up in the human face—an inexhaustible panorama to which I finally devoted myself. In order to gain experience in making portraits, I invented a little game.

Paris concierge

Till then, the crowds that flooded the subways and the parks, the buses and the boulevards, had been no more to me than a dense mass of anonymous and indistinguishable faces. What I started to do was examine each passing face. In the subway I would observe a workman sitting across from me, prostrate with fatigue. I would concentrate on one detail: eyes, for example, or else the nose, the forehead, or the chin, as if all the rest were hidden under an imaginary mask. By thus discreetly studying the faces that chance had set before me, I began to grasp the importance of detail, the symbolic essence of the individual: an imperceptible quiver at the corner of a contorted mouth, a wrinkle on the forehead, a furtive wink, a heavy eyelid. Sometimes just the expression in a man's eyes tells us more than his whole body.

Yet to my mind the most profound secrets are revealed by the mouth, for it is the most difficult part of the face to control. Look at the lips of that six-year-old child—full lips, half open: they show an absence of any distrust and a curiosity about men and things. For her the world is still filled with miracles and the unknown. The young woman sitting next to her, holding her hand, has a thin, tight-lipped mouth. The corners of her lips, drawn slightly down, express a hard life burdened with care. However rigid her bearing, she is betrayed by that detail.

The huge procession of faces that have paraded before me and which I shall never see again has made me aware of the fact that no two physiognomies are alike; indeed, it is rare to find two that are even somewhat related. A painter can take all the time he wants to immobilize the subtleties of a personality on canvas. Like a hunter, the photographer has no more than a moment; he must lie in wait for his prey and swiftly catch the revealing expression. Once the photograph is taken, he moves out of sight. Our first thought in front of a good painted portrait is to ask the painter's name. But in photography it is the model that counts, and the role of a good photographer is to be the sensitive instrument by means of which a personality is revealed.

Paris flea market

15

More on Food and Writers

Adrienne Monnier's bookshop was a privileged literary center, but her cuisine was equally renowned. I attended a few of the well-known dinner parties she gave for her friends. Adrienne was a marvelous cook and liked to eat well.

"One must prepare very simple dishes with very great care in order to keep the natural flavor of the food," she would say. "French cuisine and French fashion reign supreme in the world for similar reasons: they seek, above all, to achieve exquisite shadings; they endeavor to be subtle, discreet, delicately varied, rich in substance, and sparing of means."

Every day she would walk over to the rue de Buci market, on the other side of the boulevard Saint-Germain, for a good cook must know how to buy. She advised women to learn how to spot the characteristics of good meat, choice fowl, and delicate fish. "One should know absolutely everything about cheese, and learn to taste wines. It's not because sauces are hard to digest and fattening that one should avoid them. A superbly blended sauce is probably the highest expression of the culinary art. We all should eat one from time to time, diligently and in a state of recollection, as one reads a poem. And above all (this

93

Adrienne Monnier, rue de Buci, 1938

is my passion talking), one must be an excellent pastry cook."

She was to pay dearly for being such a gourmand: when I met her, she already had liver trouble and was on a diet.

One day in June 1936 Adrienne invited me to a dinner party she was giving in honor of T. S. Eliot, who, on a short visit to Paris, had given a poetry reading at Sylvia Beach's. The other guests were André Gide, Jean Schlumberger, Sylvia Beach, and François Valéry, the poet's younger son.

"When Gide comes to dinner at the house, something always happens. A painting falls off the wall, the lights suddenly go out, a glass breaks. He casts a spell around him," said Adrienne as she bustled about her kitchen, its walls covered with sparkling pots and pans.

"Today we shall eat very simply," she added, with a little sigh. "Gide and Schlum [as Jean Schlumberger was called by his friends], T. S. Eliot, Sylvia Beach, and I are all on diets. Only you and François can eat everything, but you're in the minority." We were the youngest. All the others were around fifty.

"There will be bouillon, then half a squab with peas for each (there's no point in serving any more, I know my guests)"— Adrienne loathed leftovers—"and a tart for dessert." There was something heroic about such moderation: Adrienne was one of the greatest gourmands in Paris.

While she continued to prepare dinner, I helped Sylvia Beach set the table. The ceilings were so low in that old house at 18 rue de l'Odéon that a tall man was in danger of bumping his head. Here, too, there were a lot of books: Adrienne's personal library, which she later left to the City of Paris. In the drawing room, large bookcases with glass doors contained rare editions, most of them dedicated to her. The Directoire or Empire furniture stood directly on the old waxed floor—Adrienne did not like rugs. The curios above the marble fireplaces created a very personal, intimate atmosphere in the spacious rooms. The pictures embroidered on silk were the work of her younger sister Marie. One depicted Rimbaud's *Drunken Boat,* and another, a tramp stretched out on a bench, a bottle of wine at his feet, under the Paris sky at night. Marie spent hours at her

T. S. Eliot at Shakespeare and Company, 1936

17

Claudel, Gide, Valéry

One never knows whether the person one has photographed will like his portrait. It may be that his friends discuss it among themselves. For some the portrait is not a good likeness; others find it a true reflection of his personality. As for the model, he almost never recognizes himself. That is because a personality is prismatic, and like a precious stone, the way it glitters depends on the facet exposed. When I presented François Mauriac with the portrait I had just made of Paul Claudel, he commented: "Never show it to him. He looks so wicked! That man can only talk to God!"

I had confidence in Mauriac; terrified by what he saw in the picture, I did not dare submit it to the model. Years later a friend asked me for it. I let him have a print, never suspecting that he would take it to Claudel to have it autographed.

"Why have I never seen this photograph?" exclaimed Claudel. "It's excellent. . . ."

However, the author of *Tête d'or* and *The Tidings Brought to Mary* did not like photographers. He had posed for only a few minutes and unwillingly. He had agreed to go along with the game at the gentle insistence of Adrienne Monnier, when talking with her one day in her bookshop.

I have always preferred to photograph a person in his own surroundings, amid his personal objects. The model then has a feeling of being in a familiar universe, which relaxes him and makes my job easier. Moreover, the way a house is decorated reflects the person who lives in it. Taking a picture of someone next to a curio he cherishes makes the photo more expressive. Of course, there are people who deliberately live in a neutral, impersonal environment. But such austere homes reveal just as much about their inhabitants as the homes of those who are flamboyant with forms and colors. Most artists create such a personal atmosphere around them that it remains engraved in one's mind. I can still see Matisse in his apartment on the boulevard du Montparnasse, its walls covered with his own shimmering paintings. I recall the picture of a woman against a bright red background; and it seems to me that that particular red has deepened and pointed up my memory of the artist. As for Bonnard, I am unable to recall him without the light and colors of the countryside which suffused his house in Le Cannet and which can be found in his canvases. When we think of someone we know, we do not see only his body and gestures; our memories evoke an object, a color, words, sometimes a smell: a whole individual geography, composed of a thousand details, condensed into a complex image.

When we happen to be disconcerted by an atmosphere, it is the shock of surprise that remains with us. I shall never forget my astonishment at discovering that Gide, the aesthete, in his spacious apartment on the rue Vaneau, had an absolutely monastic bedroom. True, Gide was an avowed enemy of objects, which did not prevent him from being particular about his physical appearance. Knowing that I made color photographs, he put a red silk scarf around his neck which was very effective against his black velvet jacket. He posed with confidence, striking studied attitudes. He insisted on being photographed next to a piece of Marie Monnier's colorful embroidery, then in front of his bookcase filled with magnificent bindings. Afterward I took him at his desk, under the death mask of Leopardi. He rested his head on his hand and seemed lost in thought. His whole person exuded extraordinary power. I caught the affinity between the mask and the contours of Gide's face—haughty and aristocratic, with its bulging forehead and sardonic mouth, a deep wrinkle at either side. That day I understood why Gide had exerted such an enormous influence on two generations—an influence that issued more from his person than from his works.

"Come along," he said suddenly. "We're going to pay a visit to Madame van Rysselberghe. You can photograph us together."

As we walked through one of the rooms, a grand piano caught my eye.

"I love music," said Gide, when he saw that I had noticed it. "I sometimes play for hours; nothing stimulates me as much as music."

I had heard from friends that he played extremely well and that Chopin was one of his favorite composers.

Madame Théo van Rysselberghe, widow of the Belgian painter, lived in an apartment on the same floor as Gide's. She was an old friend of the writer's, and her daughter Elisabeth had borne him a child, Catherine, whom he was to recognize publicly only after his wife's death in 1938. "The Little Lady," as Madame van Rysselberghe was called by her friends, was a charming old woman of about the same age as Gide. They were then both seventy. I took a series of photos of them as they drank their tea. The sitting room was filled with curios and flowers; photographs of Gide and other friends covered the desk.

"The best means of learning to know oneself is seeking to understand others," Gide wrote in his *Journal* on February 10, 1922.

In contrast to Gide, who liked to live in rather bleak surroundings, Paul Valéry, whose prose was so pure and abstract, lived in a sensual atmosphere of luxury and color, amid delightful old furniture and admirable paintings by his aunt Berthe Morisot, Odilon Redon, and Degas, who had been his friend.

As for his desk, it alone was worth a photograph. On it was a huge heap of books, boxes, papers, and tiny objects, in the middle of which the poet had contrived to make a little free space. He told me, with a shrug of the shoulders, that it was

André Gide and Mme. Théo van Rysselberghe, 1938

impossible for him to write if he did not feel surrounded by piles of papers, and that he had been reduced to typing his texts because he could no longer make out his own handwriting. He would start work very early in the morning. "Between the lamp and the sun, moment pure and profound, I write what comes of itself."

Champs-Elysées

"I have an idea," he said. "Rinette"—as Marie Monnier was
called by her friends—" you're going to make up my face; then
the photos will be perfect. Wait, I'll be back in a minute," with
which he disappeared into the bathroom, to return fifteen minutes later freshly shaved and carefully dressed.

"But Fargue, we're not making movies," I ventured to comment.

Still, the idea of being made up amused him and he stuck
to it.

I can still see the preparations being made for that memorable sitting: Fargue seated in a chair, and Rinette dusting his
cheeks with powder. The poet gave himself up to the proceed-
ings with undisguised pleasure.

When the photographs were developed, I invited him to
come and see them projected on a screen. What Fargue beheld
was a face as nebulous and wavering as a spectre evoked during
a spiritistic séance—formless and colorless, a kind of ghost
emerging from a bag of flour.

"That, Fargue, is you—with your confounded makeup," I
said. Fargue, who generally had an answer for everything, was
speechless.

"No, it's all wrong," he finally murmured.

As a matter of fact, it *was* all wrong; the whole proceeding
had to be repeated next day, but this time without makeup.

"Tell me a story, Fargue, but the minute I say 'stop,' don't
move any more!"

I wanted to get his pudgy little hands, which were so expressive. Then Fargue began to declaim like a tragedian: "The pope
is dead—the pope is dead—the pope is dead," and he moved his
hands forward, making a gesture of false compassion. Actually,
the pope had just died.

This time the result was better.

Fargue conceived a liking for me and took me under his
wing.

"Gisèle isn't beautiful," he told Adrienne Monnier, "but
she has charm."

Léon-Paul Fargue, 1948

He offered to introduce me into the "salons" to find me clients.

"Those people have the money to get themselves portrayed. Come to the Café de Flore tomorrow evening around nine. I'll take you to Madame X's and we'll see what happens."

I found Fargue sitting at a table outside. When I wanted to hail a taxi, he stopped me.

"Don't bother. Here's my own."

And, indeed, there was a taxi parked right alongside.

"I've had it since five this afternoon," he said as he hoisted himself inside.

Madame X lived in a fashionable neighborhood. Her town house was brilliantly lighted. Fargue was now almost two hours late. He had been invited for dinner, but apparently everyone was used to seeing him appear at the oddest hours. I was presented to the mistress of the house, then to a general with a huge moustache and to several young people who appeared to divide their time between diplomacy, banking, and horse racing. The drawing room was furnished in Louis XV, and I sat down, somewhat intimidated and ill at ease, on the edge of a rather uncomfortable chair. After having spent five minutes greeting everyone there, Fargue began to yawn, and seeing that I had taken refuge in a corner, he said:

"It's too damn boring. Come on, let's get out of here."

"But we just arrived!"

"Nonsense. That doesn't matter." And turning to our hostess: "Dear friend, I completely forgot that I have still another appointment. Unfortunately I have to leave you," upon which, with a wink at me, Fargue rushed to the door, all the guests gazing at him aghast. He had completely forgotten why he had asked me to accompany him.

The taxi was still in front waiting for us.

"To the Brasserie Lipp," he told the driver, lighting a fat cigar.

"See the enameling on the walls? It's the work of my father, made in his little ceramics factory. My poor father! I hardly knew him; he died when I was just a little child. Poor me, with neither

father nor mother," he suddenly concluded in a sepulchral
voice. Noticing the skeptical expression on my face, he looked
at me with eyes full of reproach.

It was past midnight when we left the restaurant. The taxi
was still waiting, and Fargue took me home. The amount on the
meter must have been fabulous: I didn't dare look.

I saw Fargue very often. The last time was eleven years after
our first meeting. It was in the spring of 1947. He was in bed,
immobilized by a stroke. His eyes had become even more
fixated. As always, the butt of a cigarette was stuck between his
lips, the ashes falling all over the place. There was a pile of books
beside him, and the blanket was hidden under a heap of papers.

"Luckily, illness doesn't prevent me from writing; but my
dear Paris, I never see it any more. Well, since I can't go out,
people come to see me." Indeed, he had visitors every day. In
spite of all, he continued to be in good spirits and smiled at his
friends. And too bad if his pajama tops were not always but-
toned!

"But Fargue," said the engraver Daragnès one day, "that's
your navel I see there!"

"Of course it's my navel; strange, it looks like an extinct
volcano."

I was soon to leave for South America.

"Don't leave," Fargue asked me. "Perhaps I'll be able to get
up in a few weeks; I'll take you to all the neighborhoods I talk
about in *Le Piéton de Paris*. I'd so much like the book to be
illustrated with color photographs. If you leave now, you'll miss
the opportunity of taking them with me, for my time is short. I
shall soon take off for regions from which one never returns."
And he pointed to the ground with his thumb.

"We who have come from ages immemorial and made our
way through so many menacing forms—dark forms left behind
us one after another, to die alone—what will remain to us when
we, in turn, have to slip through the invisible slit and, seeking
our future dwellings, continue to rise or descend?"

Fargue was not wrong. When I returned two years later, he
was no longer there. His lamp had gently gone out.

19

Colette

Colette was not concerned about looking beautiful on film. What she wanted, above all, was to fascinate. With her penetrating eyes and her studied gestures, she was a born actress who loved the lens and understood its requirements.

The first color photos I made of her were taken one morning in the spring of 1939. The windows of her apartment were wide open, overlooking the gardens of the Palais-Royal. Colette was in bed.

"I always work lying down," she told me. "I have arranged a little table which slides over the bed."

The lamp attached to the working table was covered with periwinkle-blue paper, like the sheets she used for writing. Even at that early hour her face was carefully made up. Her hair, thick and crisp, flaming red, was cut short and fell in bangs over her forehead. It framed her face, brightened by her dramatic eyes, like a crown of flames. A crimson scarf, tucked into her navy-blue dressing gown, created a symphony of color that was perfect for a photograph.

When I did her portrait, I agreed that no one would see the photographs before she herself had examined them and made her choice.

Maurice Goudeket and Colette, 1954

A few days later, she arrived at my place, accompanied by
a young man.

"Stay outside," she told him.

The two of us alone looked over the pictures. I awaited her verdict somewhat anxiously. Finally, her face lit up with a smile. She opened the door with an imperious gesture.

"Come in, Maurice . . . you can see . . ."

"Maurice" was her new husband.

Thirteen years later, in 1952, I photographed Colette a second time. She was celebrating her eightieth birthday. It was in Monte Carlo, where she was staying at the Hôtel de Paris, with its flamboyant style of decoration which recalled the early 1900s and seemed straight out of one of her novels.

"Today I have everything: friends, sympathy, and success, but I can no longer walk." Her voice was plaintive. "How I would love to be young again . . . fifty-eight . . . I was a happy and passionate woman then!"

20

James Joyce

It was in 1934 that I saw James Joyce for the first time. He was dining with his wife in a restaurant near the Gare Montparnasse. I was still a student, and Joyce was one of the literary idols of my generation. I was fascinated as I observed the tall, slim man on whom the waiter was lavishing the kind of attention reserved for celebrities.

During the last ten years of his life, in the thirties, Joyce moved in very different circles from those he had frequented in the twenties. His former friends—Ezra Pound, for example—had left Paris; and the well-known group that had gathered around F. Scott Fitzgerald and Ernest Hemingway was by then merely a legend.

In 1936 Adrienne Monnier's Maison des Amis des Livres had published my thesis in book form. I had the same publisher as Joyce! And so it was that we met that same year at one of Adrienne's dinner parties.

I believe that the main topic of conversation was the art of cooking. But I was so impressed I could hardly eat! I remember, however, that as I watched the play of shadow and light on the fine bone structure of Joyce's face, I thought of the portrait I could do of him that very moment.

During the following months I tried to persuade him to pose, but Joyce kept refusing—with the excuse that he was not feeling well, that his eyesight was troubling him, or that he had too much work to do. In the spring of 1938 he had completed *Finnegans Wake,* which was to come out simultaneously in the United States and in England. One of his closest French friends, the critic Louis Gillet, suggested that I write to him, explaining how important good photographs would be for publicizing the book. He advised me to mention my contacts with the French, British, and American press, as well as my photo-essays, which were then being published in magazines known throughout the world. In his reply Joyce said merely that he would like to see my collection of writers' portraits, and asked me to organize a slide showing at his home.

A few days later I arrived at 7 rue Edmond-Valentin, carrying a small projector, a screen, and my box of photographs. I had promised Joyce's wife, Nora, that I would not stay long, for I knew he was not well.

Joyce, half blind, sat so near the screen that he could have touched the faces of his contemporaries: Claudel, Valéry, Gide, Jules Romains, Montherlant, Aragon. During the entire showing, which lasted over an hour, he said not a word. When I turned on the lights again, I heard him heave a deep and dejected sigh. He appeared to be coming out of a dream.

"They're splendid," he said. "When do you want to photograph me? Not in color, of course. I couldn't stand the harsh lights on my eyes."

I was delighted to at least do a black and white portrait of him. We also spoke of a photo-story on "James Joyce in Paris." He had very definite ideas on how he wanted to be presented to the world press on the publication of *Finnegans Wake.* He telephoned his friend and personal adviser Eugene Jolas, publisher of the review *transition,* and asked him to come over the next day so that I could take them together, correcting the proofs of the book. He also wanted me to take a series of photographs in Sylvia Beach's bookshop, Shakespeare and Company, with Adrienne—not for old time's sake, but for practical purposes: Joyce knew that English and American readers associated him with Sylvia, who had so courageously published *Ulysses* in 1922, while French readers knew that Adrienne had published the book in its French translation. We decided to end the story with pictures of Joyce at home, surrounded by his wife, son, and grandson—the human side of this great writer, which had almost disappeared behind the smokescreen of literary criticism.

The photographs were taken in several sittings during May of 1938. Joyce was patient and very eager to get good results. When they were ready, he seemed delighted and asked me to destroy only five or six of the hundred I had taken. We then selected some twelve pictures which I distributed to the press.

Since everyone wanted the latest photographs of Joyce, I soon had the pleasure of telling him that he could count on worldwide circulation of my story.

For various reasons the publication of *Finnegans Wake* was delayed, and it was not until May 4, 1939, that it appeared simultaneously in New York and London. Early in March, *Time* magazine asked me for a color portrait of the author to use for one of its covers.

Since I had promised Joyce not to trouble him any more, I was reluctant to approach him again. But his friends thought that a *Time* cover would be great publicity for a book as difficult as *Finnegans Wake*. It was Sylvia Beach who hit on an idea. Joyce,

James Joyce, Sylvia Beach, Adrienne Monnier at Shakespeare and Company, 1939

James Joyce, with his son George, Helen Joyce,
and their son Stephen, 1939

Eugene Jolas and James Joyce, 1938

the Irishman, was not only intimately involved with his fictional characters, but superstitious as well. And it happened that my husband's name was the same as that of the hero of *Ulysses*.

"Write to him," Sylvia told me, "and sign your married name."

I could only congratulate Sylvia on the move, for Joyce accepted at once.

The sitting took place on March 8. He opened the door himself when I arrived. He had put on a wine-colored velvet jacket and was wearing several jeweled rings on his long sensitive fingers. He seemed altogether miserable at being photographed in color and kept glancing uneasily at my apparatus. His nervousness finally affected me: I began tangling up wires and dropping things; the atmosphere was getting more and more strained. Suddenly, as Joyce groped about looking for the chair I had arranged for him, he hit his head against a lamp, and cried out as if he had been stabbed, clasping his hands to his forehead.

"I'm bleeding. Your damned photos will be the death of me!" he shouted, forgetting in his pain that he had made it a rule never to swear in the presence of a lady.

"Nora, have you got some scissors?" I called out to his wife, in the next room. Gentle, motherly, and soothing, she came in and approached him as one would a frightened child. I pressed the cold steel against the almost imperceptible scratch to prevent swelling, a remedy I recalled from my childhood.

Now that he was calmer, Joyce sat down and, with a magnifying glass, began to examine the page of a book, as he so often did. I snapped a picture of him and went on to finish my roll of film as quickly as possible, before promising the ailing man that I would really never bother him again.

Visibly relieved, he kept me a few minutes more; we talked about *Finnegans Wake*, speculating on the kind of reception it would get from the critics and public. At the end his voice grew weak and tired; he spoke about death—his own death—predicting that *Finnegans Wake* would be his last book.

I assured him that after years of intense work every writer

is depressed and exhausted, that he was still young (he was only fifty-six), and that in France the "young" members of the French Academy were at least sixty. He refused to be consoled, and a touch of gloom hung over us as I left.

I hailed a taxi and asked the driver to take me as quickly as possible to the laboratory, where a technician was waiting to develop the film; the best portrait of Joyce had to be sent immediately to *Time* magazine in New York.

My driver was so anxious to do his best that, as he turned a corner, we skidded and hit another car. I was thrown forward and covered with bits of broken glass; my camera was smashed.

I arrived home with blood on my face and tears of rage in my eyes, and at once telephoned Joyce.

"Mr. Joyce," I said, weeping, "you cursed my photos; you put some kind of bad Irish spell on them and my taxi crashed. I was almost killed and your photos are ruined. Now are you satisfied?"

I heard Joyce sigh and guessed that I had not been mistaken: he must have cursed me and now felt responsible for the accident. Embarrassed, he made an appointment with me for another sitting the next day.

When I arrived, he was full of remorse and very anxious to make amends. He had put on a black velvet jacket instead of the wine-colored one, and all his rings were different. This time everything went well, and I kept him only a few minutes.

When I reached the laboratory, I was overjoyed to find that the film of the previous day had not suffered from the accident. So I had two series of color portraits.

Joyce was as happy as a child when *Time* came out with his picture on the cover, and he showed it to everyone who came to see him. Better still, he was really amused by the whole story, which he told to his friends, concluding: "I had said I would never be photographed in color. Well, I was caught by Mrs. B., not once but twice. She's even cleverer than the Irish."

21

A Testy Old Man:
G. B. Shaw

Joyce, very satisfied with my photographs, had suggested that I go to England to add a few British writers to my collection—H. G. Wells, George Bernard Shaw, Elizabeth Bowen, Vita Sackville-West, Virginia and Leonard Woolf, and others.

"Tell them that you photographed me, that I was very pleased with my portraits, and that I advised you to do theirs. They won't refuse."

It was true. All of them agreed to pose for me.

The first one I wanted to photograph in London was George Bernard Shaw. No Englishman since Shakespeare had produced such remarkable theatrical works. By giving dramatic form to the problems of his times, he exerted an enormous influence on his contemporaries. No one in the world of literature had kept the public in greater suspense. The most phlegmatic Englishmen were staggered by the violent controversies in which he became involved and by the crusades he launched against the established order. But while many saw him as a wild revolutionary, Shaw considered himself an "active evolutionist."

In his Preface to *Back to Methuselah* Shaw gave his opinion that the "human animal" was incapable of solving his own social problems, that premature death always prevented his attaining wisdom. For him, Darwin's theory of natural selection was too mechanized and accidental; creative evolution, however, rested on the idea (Shaw said the simple fact) that the human will was capable of anything if it were conscientious and convinced of the necessity of creating and organizing something entirely new. The only means by which man might realize his latent capacities was thus through the deliberate prolongation of life. Then man would find the means to abolish war and every other evil which plagued his life.

The image of Shaw, with his long white prophet's beard, had become inseparable from the intellectual landscape of the first decades of the twentieth century. One heard countless legends about him, the least offensive of which was that the irascible man was almost unapproachable. I did not dare give Joyce as a reference, for I knew the letter Shaw had sent to Sylvia Beach in 1922, when she was trying to find subscribers for the first edition of *Ulysses*.

"I have read fragments of *Ulysses* in its serial form," he wrote. "It is a revolting record of a disgusting phase of civilization, but it is a truthful one. . . . To you possibly it may appeal as art. . . . In Ireland they try to make a cat cleanly by rubbing its nose in its own filth. Mr. Joyce has tried the same treatment on the human subject. I hope it may prove successful. . . . I must add, as the prospectus implies an invitation to purchase, that I am an elderly Irish gentleman, and if you imagine that any Irishman, much less an elderly one, would pay 150 francs for such a book, you little know my countrymen."

I consulted H. G. Wells, who agreed to act as an intermediary between me and that difficult man. "Let me take care of it," he reassured me. "I'll attend to G.B.S. In fact, I'll write him a letter immediately. I shall explain to him that he must be included in your collection. You don't know how conceited he is."

Wells sat at his huge work table and filled two long pages with his careful, measured handwriting. Then he had the letter delivered. I received a reply from Shaw's secretary, giving me an appointment to come to 4 Whitehall Street the following Sunday at 6 P.M.

I arrived and was unpacking my cameras and reflectors when I suddenly realized that someone had come up behind me. It was Shaw. At that time he was over eighty. It is often disappointing to meet someone you have already formed an idea of from photographs. Yet, seeing him for the first time, face to face, it was the contrary. I found him shorter than I had expected, and of rather frail constitution, but his head was magnificent, the eyes piercingly blue and the famous white beard translucent and silky.

"Good afternoon," he said. "I hope you know your business. I warn you, I am a photographer myself and can't be fooled. Have you brought any of your pictures?"

Fortunately I had with me my photographs of André Gide, Paul Valéry, and Romain Rolland, which I showed him.

He glanced at them with absolute disdain. "They are pretty awful, don't you agree?"

I was expecting to be shown out.

"I see you use a Leica," Shaw went on. "I have the same model. I only hope you know how to use it. Now, for my portrait, you must concentrate on one thing. Don't cut off a bit of my beard. Remember. Don't cut my beard."

To my surprise, Shaw, with amazing agility, dropped to his knees.

"Now, if you take me from this angle, down here, you will get an interesting view of the beard."

At that precise moment, however, I had new worries. In England every house seems to have a different system of switches and a variety of electric currents ready to defy the average unmechanical-minded mortal like myself. I tried out a series of new contacts while Shaw paraded about the room giving me assorted bits of very useless advice. From time to time he glanced into the mirror and stroked his beard. Then, apparently satisfied at last, he sat down in the big armchair, ready to be captured for posterity. I looked through my viewer and once again was fascinated by that beautiful head, with its intelligent blue eyes. He seemed at that instant to be the reincarnation of some biblical prophet.

Here I was with one of the most extraordinary personalities of our times, a man known and admired by millions. I felt my hand tremble with nervous anticipation. This was really going to be a good picture.

"Don't cut my beard," Shaw mumbled.

"It's perfect," I answered, ready to snap. Then the tragedy occurred. Every light in the place went out, and darkness melted into silence.

"There, Mr. Shaw. You see what you have done. Your warnings and sarcasm blew the fuse."

For the first time, Shaw seemed a little remorseful.

"Something is forever happening to these lights," he grumbled. "It will probably take an hour to fix them. And what are we going to do meanwhile? I was just in the right mood to pose."

"Well," I said, as I pushed back the heavy long curtains from the window. "There's a wonderful moon out tonight. I could photograph you here with the moonlight shimmering through your beard. It would make a remarkable picture but, of course, it's impossible. You would be obliged to remain perfectly still for at least three minutes *without saying a word* . . . and you could not do that, I'm sure."

G.B.S. regained his fighting spirit. "Young lady . . . you forget I am a sportsman. Nothing is impossible for me. Take your picture."

I set up my camera on the tripod and again looked through the viewer. Shaw took his place near the open window. His entire figure was outlined by a cool blue light; behind him, one could see the faint shadows of a chimney and trees softly interlaced. He did not move. He had not a word of advice to give me now.

In less than a minute the picture was finished. Shaw appeared like a white statue, wrought from marble in the moonlight: only his intense eyes had their usual glow. I wondered just how long he would hold still. The moments seemed an eternity. At last, in compassion, I said the picture was finished. I had had

128   my little revenge. After all, he had not been much of a help to me.

Shaw seemed very satisfied with the whole affair and confident that the picture would turn out well.

"Mr. Shaw," I said, taking advantage of his change of mood. "It would be nice if you would give me the letter Mr. Wells wrote about me. I'd like to keep it as a souvenir."

"I have thrown it away," he answered dryly. "I don't keep letters."

I had the odd feeling he was afraid I'd make money out of it some day.

Shaw's picture, when developed, was everything I had hoped it would be—except for one thing. A tiny portion of the beard was cut off! In despair, I knew I could never send it to Shaw. I sent a copy to Wells, however, together with the portrait I had done of him.

A few days later, I received his reply:

Dear Madame Freund,

Thank you for the pictures. I liked the one of G.B.S. very much. As far as my own picture is concerned, frankly I do not like it at all. It is not flattering enough.

Sincerely yours,
H. G. Wells

Like everyone else, great men are hard to please.

22

Virginia Woolf

In October 1938, shortly after Munich, H. G. Wells told me he felt the future looked very bleak. "If men cannot prevent another war, the civilized world will be destroyed. We are sinking into barbarism."

Before 1938, liberal Englishmen like Wells believed in pacifist solutions. They were convinced that imperialism could be arrested without resorting to violence. They also believed that social injustice would disappear once its causes were successively eliminated.

Wells and Shaw had been among the writers most bent on formulating a social critique. They were anxious to reform the world and quite certain that man was capable of coming to terms with such changes in a peaceable way. In the fall of 1938, after the historic meeting between Hitler and Chamberlain in Munich, Wells seemed to have lost all hope.

Virginia Woolf was in a similar state of mind. I met her during those unquiet months when the English were beginning to realize that another war was inevitable. She was shattered by the prospect.

Virginia Woolf was born into the intellectual elite of the

129

middle class. Her father, Sir Leslie Stephen, a distinguished literary critic, was an apologist for modern ideas and attacked English chauvinism. Like the other members of the Bloomsbury group, Virginia Woolf considered war unthinkable and barbarous, just as she found religious faith a mere residue of primitive superstitions. The characters in her books reflected this milieu and its concerns.

For her the novelist's task consisted in giving permanence not to the external facts of existence but to elusive and complex thoughts, made up of ever-changing and multicolored images and memories.

A writer's works are an expression of his anxieties and experiences. In Virginia Woolf's novels purely cerebral life took greater and greater precedence. It was a dangerous road, for through constantly analyzing ideas and feelings, one ends by becoming defenseless in the face of outer realities. Virginia Woolf had always been subject to serious depressions and was obsessed by the possibility of losing her mind. But the bombing and destruction of the Bloomsbury house in which she and her husband had been living must have hastened her end. She committed suicide by drowning herself in the Ouse, a river just a few hundred yards from the country house in which she had taken refuge. Leonard Woolf told me that she had slipped some large stones into her pockets to be sure she would not fail. In the note she left him, she wrote: "I have the feeling that I shall go mad. I hear voices and cannot concentrate on my work. I have fought against it, but cannot fight any longer."

The impressions we form of writers' faces from their books are often inaccurate. To me H. G. Wells looked more like a country doctor than a novelist. But Virginia Woolf, frail and luminous, was the very embodiment of her prose. She was fifty-eight when I met her. Her hair was turning gray. She was tall and slender, and her features, at once sensual and ascetic, were astonishingly beautiful. Her protruding eyebrows jutted out over large serious eyes in deep sockets. Her full and tender mouth was touching in its sadness. Her very straight, delicate nose seemed fleshless. Her face, as if bathed in inner light,

The Thames

reflected both a visionary's sensibility and great sincerity. In-deed, that very reserved woman generated a captivating atmos-phere.

It was through the writer Victoria Ocampo, editor of the Argentine review *Sur,* that I made contact with the Woolfs. One afternoon in June 1939 I had accompanied Victoria to the spa-cious old house on Tavistock Square where the Woolfs were leading a very retired life. She offered us the traditional tea, in front of a fireplace in which huge logs were slowly burning. The drawing room walls were decorated with frescoes by her sister Vanessa Bell. A little dog was dozing at his mistress's feet while she smoked cigarette after cigarette, unceasingly.

I set up my screen and showed my color portraits. She was very much interested, especially in the psychological signifi-cance disclosed by each picture. When she saw the photographs of Joyce, she told us that the manuscript of *Ulysses* had once been offered to the Hogarth Press, which was owned and run by her and her husband, but that they had refused it in order to avoid legal complications, for in England the book might very well have been considered pornographic.

"We have a famous photographer in the family," she said, bringing out an album printed by the Hogarth Press. In it was a collection of portraits of scholars and writers of the Victorian era, all of them the work of Julia Cameron.

Leonard and Virginia Woolf, 1939

"She is my grandmother," added Virginia Woolf, auto-graphing it for me.

Victoria then asked her if she would not wish to pose for me. She did not accept straightaway. She had a horror of anything that might expose her private life, but the element of psychology in my work and the novelty of the color process must have impressed her. We finally agreed on an appointment for the next afternoon.

The sitting lasted two hours. Virginia Woolf submitted to all my demands. She showed me her dresses, and the two of us chose the colors. She asked me to photograph her husband as well, and at the end they posed together, the little dog at their feet. I was very happy as I left at having been able to add their pictures to my collection.

The photographs were not developed until after I returned to France. The next time I visited London, where I was caught unawares by the declaration of war, Virginia Woolf was in the country, and I had no opportunity to meet her again.

It was in the south of France that I learned of her death. I had taken refuge there while awaiting the visas I needed to leave for Argentina, where I had been invited by Victoria Ocampo. When I arrived in Buenos Aires two years later, Victoria showed me a letter Virginia Woolf had written her in a state of acute anxiety, when she was already quite ill. She strongly reproached Victoria for having urged her to pose for me. She had not seen her portraits and probably felt threatened by the idea that they might be published without her having chosen the ones she preferred. I showed Victoria all my transparencies. She was then convinced that had Virginia Woolf been able to see them, she would not have regretted her decision. Since, for technical reasons, it was impossible to publish those color photographs, I had duplicates made in black and white, and it was those pictures that traveled around the world, without anyone ever suspecting that they were copies.

When I returned to London in 1946, I showed them to Leonard Woolf. He found them very beautiful and asked me for a few prints. Each time, on subsequent trips, he received me with

The Ouse

great kindness in his office at the Hogarth Press and helped me choose writers to add to my collection. When I read the first volumes of his autobiography, a precious document on the literary era in which he was so prominently involved as publisher, writer, and last but not least, husband to Virginia Woolf, I decided to do a story on him.

Monk's House, near Lewes, in Sussex, is a very old house, dating back to the Middle Ages. The Woolfs had bought it in 1919, and until her death Virginia Woolf had spent the summer months there. Leonard Woolf first showed me a room on the ground floor with a door opening onto the large garden.

"It was here that Virginia worked. There are her table, her pen, and her inkwell."

We climbed up an extremely narrow stairway to the next floor. In a tiny sitting room he pointed out an armchair, covered with flowered chintz. "She used to sit in it after work." Then he took me to his own study, a kind of narrow corridor under the roof, an entire wall of which was covered with books, up to the ceiling. On a small table was his typewriter. He was in the process of drafting the fourth volume of his autobiography and was typing the text straight out.

Leonard Woolf, tall and thin, was extraordinarily robust and agile for his age. From his face, chiseled and furrowed by countless wrinkles, his bright, intelligent eyes looked out at me good-naturedly. He had more to show me: a few small volumes of Virginia Woolf's diaries, covered with closely written lines of small handwriting. He himself visibly enjoyed posing. I could not help but think that his wife's death had freed him of the dreadful apprehensions that had weighed on his life for so many years. Moreover, people were starting to take an interest in his own works. He had already published over twenty volumes, but while his wife was alive, his personality had been altogether eclipsed.

I sent him the photographs; he replied immediately to tell me that he found them magnificent. When I later read the fourth volume of his autobiography, *Downhill All the Way,* I was struck by his qualities as a writer—his humor, the originality of his views on men and events, and also by everything he disclosed regarding the nightmare Virginia Woolf's illness and death had been for him.

Leonard Woolf, 1965

23

Writers
in England

T. S. Eliot, whom I had met at Adrienne Monnier's, posed for
me during the summer of 1939. He was then editing the review
Criterion. I had written to him from Paris, asking for an interview.
He answered:

"I remember, of course, meeting you with André Gide in
Paris, and it would be a pleasure to see you again. I am a little
alarmed by the prospect of a colour photograph because I do
not think I have a very beautiful colour, and I am always depressed by the sight of my photographs even uncoloured. Nevertheless, if you wish to make a photograph of me and can do
it here, I am naturally flattered."

Throughout my life as a photographer, I have been struck
by the fact that most writers hate their faces. They are the first
to want the defects of their features conjured away. Yet regular
features are not what make a face particularly attractive. Tor-
tured, ravaged faces are sometimes the most beautiful to those
who know how to read them. Hasn't genius always had the most
powerful attraction?

The anxiety of the times seemed to weigh heavily on T. S.
Eliot, and his poems reflected the vision of a disintegrating
world. In his long lyrical poem *The Waste Land* he conveys

man's incapacity to dominate the civilization he had created.

His influence on the young poets of his generation, particularly W. H. Auden and Stephen Spender, was great. Toward the end of his life, he turned to Christianity, however, while those younger poets found their solution to the contemporary crisis elsewhere.

Stephen Spender was among those who were the most talked about. In 1939 he was nearing thirty. Despite the fact that he had a romantic head and the face of a dreamer—that is how my camera saw him—he did not share the romanticism of his elders. He had just published a volume of poetry, *Trial of a Judge,* in which he professed his faith in extreme left-wing politics. Spender was a member of a small group of writers that had formed around *New Writing,* a review directed by John Lehmann. Members of the group were W. H. Auden, Cecil Day Lewis, and Louis MacNeice. These young Englishmen no longer held the illusion of a peaceable salvation for Europe shared by Wells and Shaw. They understood perfectly Fascism's power of expansion; indeed, several of them had fought Fascism in the Spanish civil war.

The list of those I wished to photograph was long. Many were living in the country. Fortunately, the young Irish writer Elizabeth Bowen happened to be in London at the time and I was able to photograph her.

Stefan Zweig, of Austrian birth, had settled in London after the Anschluss, and I added his portrait to my collection. If the English had trouble contemplating the possibility of war, Zweig, convinced that he would see it break out, was in a constant state of depression and never managed to rid himself of it. In 1941 he committed suicide with his young wife in Brazil, where he had taken refuge after the defeat of France. He did not believe in the possibility of an allied victory.

Vita Sackville-West was living in Kent, in Sissinghurst Castle. She was descended from one of the most noble families of England, and it was her family background that provided the substance of her works and which inspired the novel *Orlando* written by her close friend Virginia Woolf. Vita Sackville-West's novel *Pepita* is the story of her grandmother, a beautiful Spaniard; her mother is the heroine of *All Passion Spent,* a portrayal of old age and its problems.

"One never talks about old age," she told me. "Yet it's as good a subject as any other."

Sissinghurst Castle was surrounded by an enormous flower garden. Like most of the English, Vita Sackville-West passionately loved flowers and was well known as an expert in the field. For many years she wrote a column on gardening that was published every Sunday in one of the big English newspapers.

Very tall and sunburned, wearing slacks and a huge straw hat, Vita Sackville-West seemed to embody the English gentry, except for one detail: her strong and willful features were tem-

Stephen Spender, 1939

Victoria Sackville-West, 1939

pered by warm black eyes, inherited from her Spanish grandmother. Her husband, Harold Nicolson, was carrying a shovel and a small hoe on his shoulder. He had been a diplomat, then a Member of Parliament, and was considered in his country as one of the top specialists in foreign policy. He, too, was pessimistic about the future: "War will break out before the year is up," he said.

She showed me her garden, and above all, her roses, of which she was very proud. The air was filled with their delicate fragrance. In that gentle English countryside one got an impression of eternal peace. Nothing betrayed the anxiety of those who would soon be forced to face the horrors of war.

24

War Is Imminent

During that summer of 1939 French writers were also concerned about the approaching crisis. Several of them had fought in 1914–1918; all of them had suffered from the war; no French family had been spared. The towns and villages in the east were barely reconstructed. The year before, I had been in the Vosges. Twenty years after the armistice one could still see traces of the destruction. The forests, razed by shells, had still not recovered their normal appearance. Frail trees lifted their branches to the sky in a gesture of despair and accusation. In the thickets I found old tin cans, empty and rusted. The foxholes dug by the French soldiers in 1917 were still visible. The cemeteries in the east, with their thousands of white wooden crosses, spoke harshly of the past.

With France barely on the road to recovery, everyone was again talking of war. The Parisians could still remember the bombardment of their city by Big Bertha. All the French were horrified by the prospect of a new conflagration: they had learned that modern war causes as much suffering to the victors as to the vanquished. The threat looming over the horizon weighed on everyone's mind. The writers and artists were the

143

W. H. Auden, 1963

first to become aware of it and tried to forewarn the world.

I photographed the poet and playwright Charles Vildrac, who, in his *Chants du Désespéré,* had expressed the hope that the day would come when Europe would no longer be "A display of divergent forces / But one single destiny, one love, one tree!"

Jules Romains had worked at trying to bring France and Germany together.

Jean Giono became an advocate of pacifism and a "return to the land." He lived in Manosque, in Upper Provence, where I went to photograph him. In his novels, the most famous of which are *Harvest* and *Lovers Are Never Losers,* he lyrically describes the life of the man in the fields. He was the best-known French novelist across the Rhine, and almost all his books had been translated into German. He showed me a novel that had in fact come out in Germany even before it had been printed in France.

"Look at that man," Giono told me, pointing to a peasant who was plowing his field. "He works the land; he is happy. If everyone learned how to use a spade again, the world would be more peaceful and there would be no more wars. And look at this cloth, handwoven," he continued, pointing to his suit. "It's stronger than most machine-made material. We must go back to the old trades. What ruins the man of today is the turbulent life he leads in the cities."

Our discussion was animated.

"We cannot turn back the clock," I told him. "But men must manage to dominate the machine in order to avoid dehumanization."

I admired him as a writer, but I now understood why the Nazis courted him as they did and sent him so many invitations, which delighted him but whose meaning he never grasped. I knew that the German leaders counted on reducing France to a purely agricultural economy in order to dominate the country more easily and use it as a market for their own industrial products. It seemed to me that Giono, a man of letters, was very naïve politically.

I also photographed André Breton and about a dozen sur-

André Breton, 1965

realist writers and artists who gathered round him: Paul Eluard, Louis Aragon, Max Ernst, Philippe Soupault, Benjamin Péret, Tanguy, Jean Arp, and Francis Picabia, as well as film makers and photographers like Luis Buñuel and Man Ray. From the very beginning of their movement they had believed it necessary to combine art with political action. World War I had left them profoundly disgusted with nationalism. The writers whom they considered their masters were Rimbaud, Lautréamont, Apollinaire, and Alfred Jarry, whose play *Ubu Roi*, performed for the first time in 1895, had been a prophetic and biting satire on dictatorship.

"Transform the world," said Marx; "Change life," said Rimbaud. "Those two watchwords are in fact one," affirmed Breton. But that affirmation was not enough to hold the group together. Louis Aragon, Paul Eluard, and others left the surrealist movement, influenced by the social transformations that had taken place in Russia and which seemed to promise a more just world.

Jean Giono, 1939

25

A Memorable
Show

My collection was now substantial, and every model was curious about how I had dealt with the others. Adrienne Monnier therefore decided to invite all her friends to the shop for a private slide showing. It took place one Sunday afternoon in 1939.

The bookshop, which had been the scene of so many memorable literary gatherings, was once again transformed into a lecture hall. We rented fifty chairs, and the bookshelves were hidden behind wrapping paper, for Adrienne was afraid that certain of her guests might be tempted to help themselves. I set up my projector at the back of the hall, and at the place where Adrienne had her desk we made a rudimentary screen out of a bed sheet.

Adrienne had had a small handbill printed up to announce the showing and to serve as my advertising. The fact was, my color photographs entailed considerable expenses. I could not sell them to newspapers and magazines, which were without the means to reproduce them, and all those writers and artists had been photographed free of charge, out of friendship. The undertaking had proved to be quite a burden, with color film costing far more than the ordinary black and white. Adrienne's handbill read:

STUDIO DES AMIS DES LIVRES

Gisèle Freund

Specialist in color-photography portraits.
Continuous exhibition of writers' portraits.
(copies on paper and slide projections)

Then came the list of the portraits I had done.

At 3 P.M. the shop was filled, and I had trouble clearing a path to the projector, which I was operating myself. I was worried. In the case of a writer, for whom direct contact with the public is almost impossible, a portrait assumes great importance. He knows that the public is curious about his face, and he, of course, wants to make a good impression. Would they accept my translations? I had sought, not to endow them with the beauty of movie stars, but to immobilize, on film, "that double, which is our temperament, and those strange currents called feelings, which flow just under the surface of our physiognomy," in the words of Henri Michaux.

Paul Valéry, who was on a lecture tour in England, had delegated his wife and his son François to attend. André Gide, who was in Egypt, was represented by his daughter Catherine and Madame Théo van Rysselberghe; they were in the first row, next to Georges Duhamel and Jean Paulhan. Jules Romains, Léon-Paul Fargue, Jules Supervielle, Charles Vildrac, Jean Cassou, Jean Prévost, his wife (Marcelle Auclair), and some twenty others, accompanied by friends and family, also attended the showing. The surrealists were represented by André Breton. Louis Aragon, Elsa Triolet, and Paul Nizan, author of *La Conspiration*, formed a group of extreme left-wing writers. Jean-Paul Sartre had come with his mother, who was a head taller than he, and Simone de Beauvoir. There were also some well-known art critics and society people: I noticed the Duchesse de la Rochefoucauld next to Julien Cain, director of the National Library, and finally, Jean Genet and Maurice Sachs.

One after another the photographs flashed by. Those portraits, considerably enlarged by the projector, which did not

Romain Rolland

Marcel Duchamp

André Malraux

André Gide

Pierre Bonnard

Henri Matisse

François Mauriac

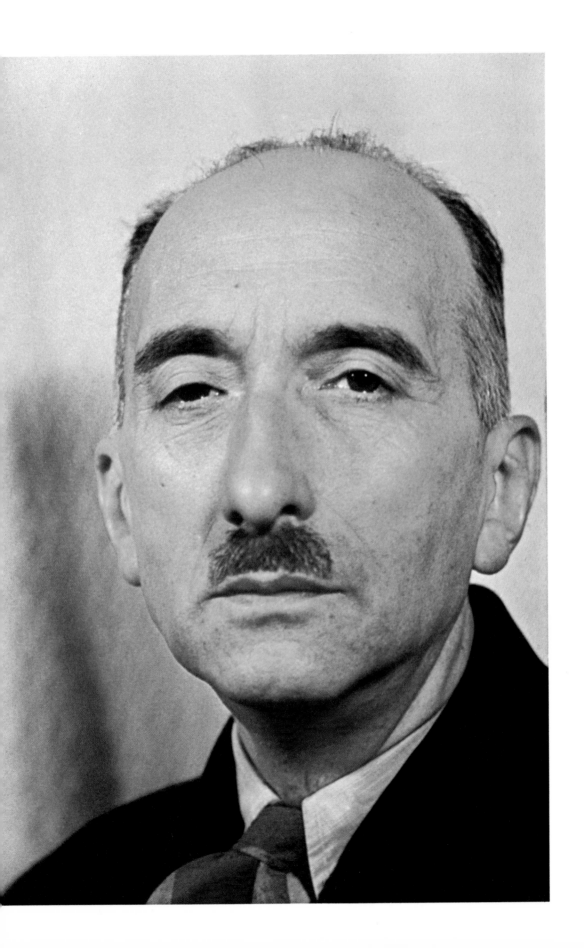

Colette

conjure away one skin blemish, were frightfully realistic. Georges Duhamel heaved a great sigh:

"I should have shaved more carefully that day!"

"If you don't find yourself photogenic," shouted Léon-Paul Fargue, "your tie surely is." It was crimson. I remembered that he had come to the house with a collection of ties in his arms. By common consent, we had chosen the one that appeared on the screen.

"This is all I can show you of Roger Martin du Gard," I announced, flashing the reproduction of a telegram on the screen:

17 February 1939, Nice

NOTHING DOING, THANKS, REFUSAL AND REGRETS STOP ABSOLUTELY POINTLESS FOR MADAME PHOTOGRAPHER TO MAKE TRIP STOP DECIDED TO TAKE MUG INTO GRAVE, LEAVING NO TRACE REGARDS

Martin du Gard

"André Breton looks like an archangel," said Adrienne Monnier.

The original, his arms folded across his chest and his head thrown back slightly, did not say a word.

"Why didn't you photograph me twenty years earlier?" murmured François Mauriac.

André Maurois also had some regrets: "You should have taken me in my academician's uniform. It's far more photogenic than I am."

"Don't come before three in the afternoon," Jean Cocteau had insisted. "I never get up before then." And there he was on the screen, his eyes lost in a dream world, around him the surrealist decor he had devised for his home.

When the showing was over, a grayish light filtered into the bookshop and discussions began. Most of the writers thought I had done very successful portraits of the others, but when it came to their own, they were of quite a different opinion. Here again was evidence of how unfit we are to combine our two

150   images: the image we have of ourselves and the one we present to others, which is the reflection of our personality as they perceive it.

"We all look as if we'd just come back from the war," said Jean-Paul Sartre as he was leaving. Prophetic words. A few months later, tragedy was upon us. All who had attended the showing would suffer from it; some would be deported, others killed.

26

Again a Refugee

The declaration of war caught me in England, and it took me a few months to get back to Paris. Many Parisians, in fear of the bombings, had left for the country. The city had a Sunday sadness about it. Stores were closed, their owners mobilized. My husband was at the front. The Ministry of Information, run by Jean Giraudoux, gave me a press card, but there was almost nothing to do: the papers published only military news. In America, however, people were still taking an interest in Paris events, and *Life* magazine commissioned me to do a color story on fashion and the big dress designers. That industry, too, was affected by the war: the dresses were short and tailored.

Jean Prévost, who was on a short leave from the front, let me do a portrait of him in his officer's uniform. With his wife, Marcelle Auclair, of Chilean descent, he had translated García Lorca and the famous Argentine writer Ricardo Guiraldes. Prévost was full of courage and hope; a few years later he died fighting in the Vercors. His comrades in the underground told me that he had tried to divert them by giving them courses in literature.

The American magazine *Time* asked me for a portrait of

General Gamelin, chief of staff of the French army, but no sooner had I taken the photograph than he was relieved of his command. Events were moving fast. On June 10, 1940, the government left Paris. Three days later, directly before the German troops arrived, I left at dawn on a bicycle—the trains were no longer running. On the rack I had attached my little suitcase, the same one I had brought with me to Paris seven years before. I found asylum in a small village in the Dordogne. Several weeks later, I was informed that my husband had been made a prisoner of war. He got word to me that he would try to escape and succeeded a few months later. I met him in the still unoccupied part of France. He told me he would go back to Paris to fight the Germans in the Resistance, and advised me to leave the

French troops on the Champs-Elysées, 1939

country as soon as possible. Being of German origin, undoubtedly listed by the Gestapo, and now the wife of an escaped prisoner as well, I actually feared for my life. Victoria Ocampo obtained an Argentine visa for me, but it took over a year to procure the papers necessary to reach the banks of the Rio de la Plata. It was the second time in my life that I had to begin a new existence, only this time I went armed: I was proficient in a trade.

I had dreamed of making long journeys, but had never left Europe. My departure for Argentina was the beginning of a new experience. Until then I had specialized in portraits, but I had only one means of getting to know the American continent: becoming a photo-reporter.

27

Buenos Aires

The very first impression of a foreign country or city is always disappointing. Arriving in London by train, one spends an hour riding through sad, gloomy suburbs, full of small brick houses blackened by soot. The outskirts of Paris are not any cheerier. When I arrived in Buenos Aires by ship, the first things I saw were endless docks, men unloading trucks, and smoking freighters.

The immigration officer carefully examined my papers:

"You're French and you are an artist by profession?" He was looking at me rather oddly. "What kind of artist?"

"An artist-photographer, if you don't mind."

"Better change the term: a lot of French women who enter the country as 'artists'—well, you know . . ." he said, making an unambiguous gesture, "they're in what you'd call a particular profession."

The other employees began to smile. I thought of Albert Londres's book, *Le Chemin de Buenos Aires,* on the white slave trade in South America. It was a chapter in Argentina's past, but one that must have left its traces.

Buenos Aires.

The streets are straight and the clamor deafening. There are miniature buses called *collectivos*, cumbersome trolleys, and taxis, all of which are driven at breakneck speed and stop only when a passenger shouts "esquina," meaning "corner," which signifies: "I want to get out at the next street corner." The city is huge, white, and modern; squares and luxuriant parks relieve its congestion; the window displays convey the country's opulence.

Florida Street is its main thoroughfare, as well as the center of elegance. Here one finds all the big stores, the art galleries, the largest bookshops, the finest jewelers, the fashion houses, the innumerable shoe and leather-goods stores. The street is narrow and clogged by an uninterrupted, massive stream of pedestrians. The crowd is polyglot, but those one would take for Englishmen, Frenchmen, Spaniards, Italians, Germans, or other Europeans are all Argentineans.

When I met an Argentinean, he would always turn out to be the son of Spaniards, or Italians, or be of French, German, English, or some other extraction. Never was he an Argentinean of long standing. Indeed, almost the entire Argentinean population is of recent European descent. The Indians who, before the Spanish conquest, peopled the Rio de la Plata basin or the vast stretches of the Pampas and Patagonia have almost completely disappeared.

The descendants of the first Spanish conquerors, who still have some Indian blood in their veins, have an originality and exotic grace that one encounters only in Spanish-American countries. Since there are so few of them, they are lost in the heterogeneous mass of the descendants of those who disembarked in Argentina between 1880 and 1909. At that time a policy of massive immigration was necessary to populate that vast wilderness; but most of the immigrants settled in Buenos Aires and in the towns.

It is this cosmopolitan crowd which is responsible for Buenos Aires' physical appearance and which has made it into an essentially mercantile and incredibly variegated city. One house is built in the style of the French eighteenth century; its neighbor is pure Spanish in style; farther on is an example of 1928 German architecture; the large office building across the street is Scandinavian; and the adjacent town house was inspired by Italian architecture.

The writer Martinez Estrada called Buenos Aires "Goliath's head." It is a huge city, but as soon as one goes out into the surrounding countryside, one can travel hundreds of miles without meeting a soul.

The inhabitants of Buenos Aires have at least one thing in common: they are all *porteños*. *Porteño* comes from the word *puerto*, meaning "port." People of the port. The port of Buenos Aires is enormous, with docks stretching along the entire city from east to west, from the poor neighborhoods to the rich. The Rio de la Plata, whose waters are silvery in the wealthy suburb of San Isidro but brownish and muddy within the city, is a river in name only, for it is so wide that one bank cannot be seen from the other. It flows, dreaming of a destiny forever frustrated: it would have been a sea were it not composed of fresh water. At San Isidro it is flecked with small sailboats, and at Avellaneda, a huge suburb of slaughterhouses and factories, it breaks up into

Calle Florida, Buenos Aires

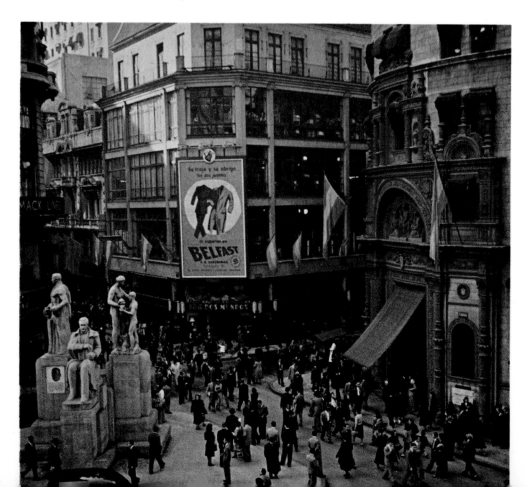

numerous brackish canals, filled with the carcasses of ships.

The inhabitant of the squalid corrugated-iron house in the Boca district is just as much a *porteño* as the owner of the town house on the Avenida Alvear.

The *porteño,* like the New Yorker and the Parisian, is a particular type. The first thing a foreigner notices is that there are very few old people in the streets. Buenos Aires is a city of youths, predominantly masculine and sporting small moustaches in the style of Douglas Fairbanks.

The two biggest diversions of the *porteño* are movies and soccer. A whole street is reserved for movie theatres, and they are diversified enough to appeal to every taste. Some are luxurious and air-conditioned in summer; others, more unassuming, show mostly national films. Certain of them specialize in dramas, adventure stories, or mysteries. At about midnight the crowds around the exits are so dense that one can hardly press forward.

In South America the passion for soccer is absolutely frenetic. It is the favorite sport of all young people, and in Buenos Aires they are in the majority. From Monday to Wednesday the subject of all their conversations is the match of the previous

Piazza San Martin, Buenos Aires

Sunday, and from Wednesday to Saturday, the match scheduled for the following Sunday. But a soccer match is an exclusively masculine entertainment, and all my friends advised me against attending one.

"It's not the type of show for a woman. But if you're really bent on going, you must reserve a seat in the official stand or in the one for ladies."

What interested me were "the people's stands."

The Palermo stadium, one of the largest in the world, can hold over 100,000 people. The games begin around three in the afternoon. When I got there at about one, an enormous mob was already crowding through the entrances to the people's stands, for the seats are not numbered. The ticket collector looked at me apprehensively.

"Señora, I advise you not to go up."

"I am a journalist and I'm not alone. I have friends with me."

He shrugged his shoulders and let us through. My two Argentinean friends, both men, put me between them, and we began to climb the large stairway. A stinking liquid was streaming down the steps, and all the men around me had rolled up the cuffs of their trousers: it was urine.

"Thousands of men come here as early as eleven in the morning in order to get a good seat. There are, of course, about a dozen toilets up there, but they are rarely used, as you can see. Now you understand."

The stands were indeed already filled with people. Today the contest was between two well-known teams: Riverplate and Boca.

Imagine thousands of men crushed against each other like sardines in a can. The people's stands—there were several of them—were separated from one another by impassable pits.

"That's in order to separate the rooters for the contending ball clubs—to avoid the danger of brawls. We're sitting with the rooters for Boca; if Riverplate scores a point, don't clap, whatever you do, or you'll be deluged with insults."

Barbed wire had been placed along the bottom of the peo-

Palermo stadium, Buenos Aires

ple's stands in order to prevent the crowd from rushing out onto
the field. Behind the barbed wire stood the firemen, ready to
spray the spectators and cool down any excessively ardent pas-
sions. Nothing but men: workmen, office workers, peons in *bom-
bachas* (a kind of baggy trousers), and above all, thousands of
young people under twenty, badly dressed, who had come from
the suburbs.

It was a fine day and the sun blazed relentlessly. In our
stand many of the spectators, as a protection, wore little paper
caps with "Boca" printed on them (they were on sale at the
entrance for only a few centavos); others simply knotted a hand-
kerchief around their necks.

Suddenly I saw little balloons floating above me.

"Don't look at them," Carlos whispered in my ear. "They're
contraceptives, blown up and launched over into the official
stands."

Finally, it was announced over a loudspeaker that the game
was about to begin. The crowd sat down.

I was leaning against a gate, observing the spectators. Argentineans have hot temperaments. The expressions on their
faces—now of despair, now of delight—their raised arms, and
their outstretched hands or clenched fists conveyed to me everything that was happening on the field, second by second. All of

a sudden the huge stadium was shaken by a deafening explosion, as if lightning had crashed down on it: thousands of spectators had risen to their feet and were roaring. This was followed by an interminable period of clapping, which gave the impression of torrential rain pouring down after an electrical storm. Clusters of men were singing and swaying wildly back and forth. Boca had scored a goal.

I then went down to the field to follow the game more closely from the spot reserved for press photographers. From there one also had a general view of the crowd, which resembled an infinite sea of black dots, buffeted from time to time by a raging wind. The echo of its screams recalled the rumble of an erupting volcano. The crowd was like a wild animal, ready to devour you. I was suddenly afraid of those unloosed masses. On the other hand, even for someone as uninitiated as myself, the flexibility, the skill, and the speed of the Argentinean players were staggering.

We left ten minutes before the end so as not to get caught in the mob. Apparently spectators were sometimes crushed to death at the exit of the stadium. We were not the only ones to be apprehensive: the long line of waiting buses had already been stormed, with clusters of men hanging onto the outside platforms at the risk of being hit by passing cars. Some were even on the roofs. The streets were congested for several miles around. It was not until about eight in the evening that my friends managed to drop me home.

28

A Citizen
of the World:
Victoria Ocampo

A few days after my arrival in Buenos Aires I asked a taxi driver to show me the town. I then realized that the most beautiful districts had been designed by French architects and that the parks had been copied from the Bois de Boulogne.

When the tour was over, the driver said: "Señora, now that you have seen the beauties of our city, I'm going to show you its ugliest house," and he dropped me in front of the house I was living in, Victoria Ocampo's, which had been built by one of Le Corbusier's disciples. Victoria later told me that the municipal officials had sued her because of it. Yet here in Argentina everything that came from France had more dazzling appeal than the French ever suspected. Literature, the arts, and fashion were received with veneration. Most of the books used in the universities, especially those on medicine, were French. But after World War II, when a steel belt was drawn around France during the German occupation, her influence began to decline. Anglo-American propaganda assumed the offensive, and for want of any alternative, the Argentineans gradually turned toward America and England.

After the collapse of 1940, the Argentinean intellectuals were extremely concerned about the fate of the French, but

161

news was rare. It was then that Roger Caillois launched his *Lettres Françaises*—the most important literary publication in the French language printed on the American continent—to which the best writers in exile were attracted. The review was financed by Victoria Ocampo.

Of Basque and Spanish extraction, with a bit of Irish blood, Victoria belonged to one of the wealthiest families in Argentina. She had spent part of her youth in France and told me that when her parents traveled to Europe, they would take with them not only all their children and several servants but also a cow, in order to have fresh milk on the ship. That struck me with wonder.

"When I learned to read, it was from a French primer." The love of France she had conceived in her earliest youth was virtually a part of herself. "When I am not in France, I try to bring France to Argentina, for the simple reason that I cannot do without it," she told members of the P.E.N. Club during a dinner given in her honor. She wrote almost all her articles and essays in French—and in the purest French. She was equally at

Victoria Ocampo, 1944

ease in Spanish, English, and Italian: she was a citizen of the world. She was also extremely beautiful. Her numerous friends included Paul Valéry, Aldous Huxley, Rabindranath Tagore, Count Keyserling, and Igor Stravinsky. In 1931, in Buenos Aires, she had founded the literary review *Sur,* which not only launched a whole generation of Argentinean writers and poets, and published the best literary works produced on the American continent, but also brought the great European writers to the attention of America. *Sur* had given Victoria Ocampo international prestige; by 1970, however, *Sur,* as a result of the economic crisis in Argentina, was being issued only twice a year.

Victoria was at the center of the Argentinean intellectual elite, which, every Sunday afternoon, would flock to her old family house in San Isidro, surrounded by a huge park of eucalyptus trees. It was there that I met and was able to photograph the most remarkable of the Argentinean writers and artists—Jorge Luis Borges, Edouardo Mallea, Martinez Estrada, Adolfo Bioy, Manuel Mujica Lainez, Ernesto Sabato, Maria Rosa Oliver, Gloria Alcorta, and many others.

Martinez Estrada, 1944

Jorge Luis Borges, 1944

29

Journey
to the End
of the Earth

I could have earned a great deal of money in Buenos Aires by photographing Argentinean high society. Thanks to Victoria Ocampo, all its doors were open to me. But to satisfy that type of clientele, there or anywhere else, I would have had to comply with its taste and do retouching, which is precisely what I had always refused to do as a means of earning my living. I preferred to travel and do photo-stories, at the risk of less security.

One place intrigued me: Tierra del Fuego, situated at the extreme southern point of the American continent, belonging half to Argentina and half to Chile.

Since Charles Darwin's famous book *The Voyage of the Beagle,* Tierra del Fuego has been thought of as an accursed region. Darwin described it as ". . . a broken mass of wild rocks, lofty hills, and useless forests . . . viewed through mists and endless storms. . . . [It is] one of the most inhospitable countries within the limits of the globe. . . . In this extreme part of South America, men exist in a lower state of improvement than in any part of the world." Darwin's notes were written over a hundred years ago, but since few travelers have ever troubled to verify his impressions, the country has kept its dismal reputation.

165

Fishermen at Tierra del Fuego

In addition to my personal belongings, I decided to pack a camp bed, a sleeping bag, an assortment of medicines, three cameras, a movie camera, a stock of film, and a small revolver.

There are several ways of reaching Tierra del Fuego. One can fly from Buenos Aires or take one of the few small ships that sail over the Atlantic to the little town of Ushuaia, until recently an Argentinean penal settlement. One can also cross the Andes and take a Chilean ship that, by way of the Pacific, goes to Punta Arenas, the southernmost town on the Chilean side. I opted for the latter.

It was in February, right in the middle of the South American summer, that I disembarked in Punta Arenas, which, with its red roofs, resembled a small town in Denmark or Sweden. The population was almost entirely of German or English extraction. The huge *estancias,* with their hundreds of thousands of sheep, were generally administered by the English.

For the first time, I caught a glimpse of Tierra del Fuego, "Land of Fire." I had expected to see an island enveloped in a red halo; then I remembered that Magellan had given it its name because of the innumerable torches which the Indians kept burning on the little boats that plowed its countless channels. But all I could see of the other side of the strait, some eight miles away, was a long black strip.

Only one Chilean ship made the crossing once or twice a year to furnish the lighthouses with supplies and to take aboard the bales of wool exported by the few stock farms. On my arrival, I learned that the ship had run aground in the Strait of Magellan, and no one knew when it would arrive.

While waiting, I visited several *estancias.* They are at least thirty miles apart; the roads connecting them, sometimes merely sheep tracks, are very difficult to drive on.

In a desert landscape, against a boundless horizon, rose a wooden house—the home of Mr. Morrison, director of the Bosis *estancia.* He had been there for twenty-three years, isolated from the world. He was a bachelor. "A woman," he told me, "would find the solitude unbearable." He was a man of about fifty, tall, with a face chiseled by the wind. His house was extremely comfortable. He put a fine room and bath at my disposal. In a country where one's nearest neighbor is so far away, hospitality is the rule. In the evening Mr. Morrison wore a dinner jacket; at the end of the world he continued observing the traditions of his ancestors. Shortly after dinner, we settled down in the drawing room, near a fireplace filled with huge burning logs.

"I run a middle-sized stock farm," he said. "Five hundred horses, a little over three hundred thousand sheep, and some hundred farm laborers. The Menendez-Behéty *estancias* have several million sheep. They are 'the Kings of Patagonia.'"

It was difficult for me to imagine thousands of those animals. In Europe we count them by hundreds. On the road I had encountered such an enormous flock that it seemed to fuse into what looked like a huge cloud of dust. The car came to a dead stop. Sheep are so easily frightened that at the slightest obstacle they panic and scatter in every direction so that it takes days and days to gather them together again.

I got another glimpse of the inland regions when I visited two homesteaders, husband and wife, who had settled down at the foot of Mt. Payne, a rocky mountain surrounded by lakes and crowned by an enormous glacier. There, the only available means of transportation was a horse. Fortunately, the Indian saddle, made of sheepskin, is very soft. They tied my legs around the horse with a lasso, for I had had polio as a child and lost the strength in my hips.

For hours we crossed arid and undulating steppes, then virgin forests through which the horses made their way step by step, along a path that was barely marked out, jumping over huge tree trunks. In single file we rode along terrifying chasms. Part of the forest had been burned by the Indians to create pastures. Black, charred tree trunks, in grotesque shapes, rose on the dizzying slopes. We crossed the rivers on horseback, for the animals were accustomed to such nautical feats.

Around noon we stopped to eat *asado,* pieces of meat placed over a fire on spits. We took advantage of the opportunity to warm up a bit, for in spite of the sun, the air was frosty.

In the afternoon we hunted wild duck and hare, which were

OPPOSITE TOP: *Petrified trees at the Straits of Magellan*

OPPOSITE BOTTOM: *Patagonia*

Patagonia

in great profusion. The animals are so unaccustomed to seeing men that they came up to us trustfully. At the end of half an hour we counted about thirty hares and the same number of birds. It was in fact more like slaughter than hunting.

Finally, in March, which corresponds to the beginning of the southern hemisphere's fall, the *Micalvi* made its appearance in the harbor. The arrival of a ship was such an event that the whole town rushed out to greet the captain and crew. Before I could embark, the Chilean authorities had me sign a paper stipulating that I was making the journey at my own risk, for navigation in the Fuegian channels was so dangerous that every crossing was an adventure.

Three days later we weighed anchor. At midafternoon it was already dusk. As the ship sailed slowly out of the harbor, the huge disk of the sun was sinking into the blackish water. On the deserted beaches and rocks were thousands of black dots: birds. The sky, covered with strangely elongated clouds, began to light up a blood-red. As night descended, the enormity of the Pampa faded as the land and water seemed to merge.

The deck was flooded with dirty, slimy water, and my traveling bag changed color while being transferred from the gang-

The Micalvi

Patagonia

plank to the cubicle in the hold where I was to spend several weeks. It was the only cabin on the ship that was arranged for passengers and was pompously called the *departamento*, although it had no porthole, no running water, and its sliding door, once closed, had a tendency never to open again. Therefore a curtain was hung in its place, separating me from the kitchen where the passengers' meals were prepared. There were about eleven of us in all, the others being farm laborers and gold diggers. They were all crammed into another cubicle, where they slept on the floor.

The *Micalvi* was a 300-ton freighter only twenty-six feet wide. The crew consisted of thirty-eight sailors, three officers, and the captain. Their average age was twenty-two, for one has to be young and hardy to confront the climate and dangers of those regions. Every Chilean sailor who wants to be promoted must make at least one trip around Cape Horn.

All through the night the ship rolled and pitched. I heard the frightened bleating of sheep (there were some thirty of them) every time a wave broke over their heads: they were crammed together at the bow of the ship. One of them was to be killed each day, and along with some canned foods, they were our only sustenance for weeks on end.

The next morning I realized that the weather had become worse. The officers were wearing heavy, hooded, camel's-hair jackets. We were traveling through a wild and austere region. On each bank was an impenetrable forest that ran along the slopes of mountains, their peaks covered with perpetual snow. One could make out transparent green-blue glaciers spread out like huge fans. The lowering sky was gray. Boundless solitude brooded over that dismal landscape, so infinitely sad, without even the chirp of a bird. It is hard to imagine human beings managing to live in such hostile natural surroundings.

Padre Torre, a Salesian missionary who was undertaking the journey in order to visit the Yahgan Indians on Navarino Island, had already lived among them for some time. Despite the fact that he was sixty-seven and had a big belly, he was extraordinarily robust. He had the square head of a Lombard peasant,

Padre Torre

with cropped white hair. His face was deeply lined, and his small
blue eyes, though shining with an unshakable faith, were mischievous. Over his cassock he was wearing a cotton shepherd's smock.

"In 1940 I lived among the Alacalufs for the first time," he told me. "They're the most primitive Indians in all South America. I was the first missionary to try the experiment. One fine day I boarded a ship like this one, which crossed the Strait of Magellan. I was put ashore at a completely wild and forsaken spot. It was as cold and humid as it is now."

We walked along the deck. In spite of my sheepskin jacket, my high boots, and all the woolens I had on, I was chilled to the bone. Beside us a sailor kept sounding to ascertain the depth of the water to avoid the many reefs in the area.

"The Alacalufs," said the priest, "are in the habit of moving about with their families. They're nomads. Every man has his

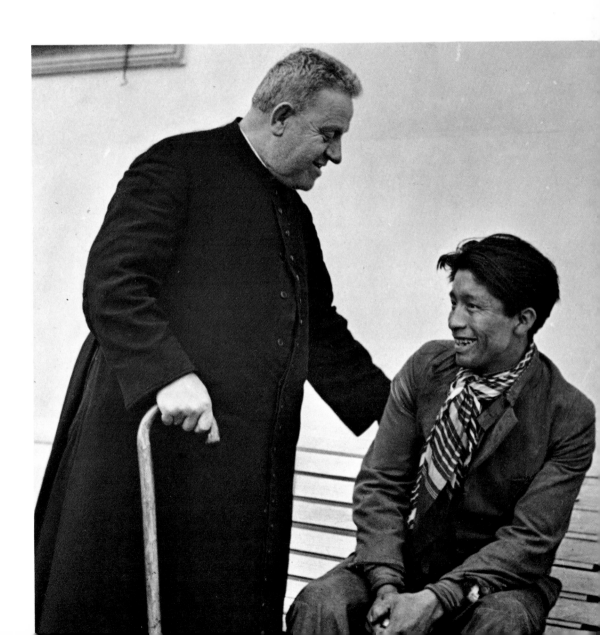

canoe. They live on the water the whole day, hunting otter and sea lions. At dusk they come ashore on the nearest bank and spend the night in a *ruca*—a few sticks joined together in the shape of a tent, on which they throw some skins. In the middle of the *ruca* a fire is lit, on which the women cook, their food consisting of fish and mussels. After their meal they sleep in the greatest promiscuity—and completely naked," he added with a sigh. "I did everything I could to teach them to wear clothing, but I could never make them understand that they ought also to be covered at night. They protect themselves from the cold and rain by smearing their bodies with whale blubber; you can imagine the stench. It's impossible to breathe inside a *ruca:* crammed into that tiny space are people, dogs, garbage, and excrement. But they've progressed. I married them like Christians; I taught them the basic rules of hygiene, as well as religion and the national anthem; you should hear them sing it!"

"They're savages," said the captain, who had joined us. "They smashed the windowpanes of the St. Peter's lighthouse, and every time the panes were replaced, they persisted in breaking them again. And you, Father, what have you to say about those who attacked the lighthouse keepers?"

"But hadn't the lighthouse keepers carried off their women and sent them back with venereal diseases?" countered the priest. "One must educate those Indians and instill faith into them, instead of teaching them to love alcohol and tobacco. They bartered precious otter skins, the fruit of several months of hunting, for one bottle of bad *caña*. They were taken advantage of and ill used. They realized it and took their revenge."

"There's some truth in what you say," admitted the captain, "but the civilization you want to bring to them harms them as well. You give them clothing, but they don't know how to use it. They never take it off, in spite of continual rainstorms. They were in better health when they were completely naked, protected from bad weather by whale blubber; now almost all of them are tubercular. The Alacalufs, that race whose origins no scholar has ever been able to trace, are almost extinguished. They are a very small people; only their torsos are normally developed. They look like the shriveled, rickety trees one sees growing along their channels."

"I taught them to believe in God," the padre continued, "but just imagine: one day, to show me that they had really understood my lessons, they made the sign of the cross, saying, 'In the name of the Father, the Son, and the good Captain, Father Torre, amen.' I had trouble convincing them that I was merely God's representative on earth, and that they shouldn't include me in their prayers. If they're very distrustful of the whites, it's because they have not forgotten certain unpleasant experiences. For example, a ship comes by. Since they are mad for sweets, they're eager to swallow the candies thrown to them by the crew. But those candies are wrapped in cellophane! When they get back on the beach, they begin to writhe in pain. As a purge, I once gave them large glasses of water in which I had dissolved some soap. The results were radical. From that day on, their confidence in me knew no bounds."

The priest rubbed his hands together as he thought back on that story, and the captain smiled at the idea of such curious medical remedies.

One of our ship's missions was to drop off provisions and take on wool at the Piedra *estancia* on Picton Island, the southernmost estate in the world. For three days now the *Micalvi* had been cruising in the vicinity without being able to cast anchor near the *estancia,* whose own harbor was inadequate. An infernally strong wind was blowing from the southwest. From time to time huge waves broke over the deck. At nightfall we entered a natural harbor facing Picton Island. The captain ordered the crew to keep the engines going all night and to remain at their stations—a wise precaution, for around five in the morning the moorings gave way and the vessel began to drift. The captain then decided to seek refuge in a safer harbor on the other side of the island. We sailed very near the house and suddenly saw a fragile little boat aimed directly at us, despite the raging wind. It was Don Faustino, the *estanciero,* who wanted to get to us at any price.

One can imagine what the arrival of the *Micalvi* meant in

Before a ruca, *Tierra del Fuego*

such remote regions. Theoretically, the ship was to stop there twice a year, but this was its first visit in over ten months. For Don Faustino and his family, the ship was their only contact with the outside world: it meant provisions, letters, and the possibility of talking to other men.

Don Faustino finally managed to come aboard. The captain embraced him warmly, and the entire crew pressed around him. He was a vigorous little man, with a very round head under his beret. His eyes never stopped smiling. He knew almost every member of the crew, with whom he was extremely popular, for he always made them a gift of some live sheep, which added pleasantly to the ship's food reserves.

We now had the wind aft, and the ship sailed ahead at unusual speed, accompanied by two porpoises. We saw them emerge one after the other to the right and left of the vessel.

Around noon we entered Banner Bay, which was the best harbor in the region. On a rock near the beach was a large painted inscription: BIG BELLOW GO TO SPANIARD HARBOUR, MARCH 1851. The captain seized the opportunity to tell me about the tragedy that had occurred in this solitary bay over a hundred years ago. Allen Gardener, a pioneering Protestant missionary, had come in December 1850 to civilize the Fuegian Indians. At the time the island was populated by a large number of Yahgan tribes. Constantly persecuted by the savage Indians, Gardener and his companions had forsaken the bay and, with their ship *Big Bellow*, had taken refuge in Spaniard Harbour, a deserted spot on the south side of Tierra del Fuego. It was not until January 1852 that a frigate which had left England to give them assistance discovered the pathetic inscription. Meanwhile, Gardener and his five companions, after a desperate struggle against the elements, had all starved to death.

During the night the wind subsided, and very early in the morning the sky was completely blue. Through the transparent water one could perceive a labyrinth of gulfweed, spreading out its brown and speckled branches. This type of algae, extremely prevalent in the Fuegian channels, has a round and viscous stem about one-third of an inch in diameter, and may grow to a length

of more than 150 feet. Its image, multiplied by the vibration of the water, resembled thousands of intertwined snakes.

Once a week I would communicate with the French consul in Punta Arenas by radio. This time I learned that *Life* magazine had telegraphed, asking me to photograph the Japanese submarines likely to be hiding in those regions. The supposition made me smile: all the Fuegian channels are full of reefs, and the only traces of boats in the area were the carcasses of ships that had run aground.

"We'll perhaps be around for a while," the captain told Don Faustino, having just received a one-sentence radio message: "Cyclone from Pacific sweeping through southern zone." And indeed, the lull did not last long.

"Look at Beagle Channel. It's covered with white foam. That means strong winds. When will we be able to load the wool and discharge provisions? Maybe tomorrow; maybe in two days. God only knows."

"In that case," replied Don Faustino, "put me ashore here. I have already spent one night on your ship and my wife must be worried. It will take me four hours at most to walk across the island. And if the Señora would like to come with me," he added, "it would be a nice change for her after the *Micalvi*'s decks."

Ever since the trip began, I had wanted to do only one thing: explore the islands covered with what seemed like impenetrable forests. I therefore jumped at the chance. We had to leave immediately, for it was almost two in the afternoon and the southern days are short.

"My wife is going to be so pleased! It isn't often that she has a guest, especially a woman!" said Don Faustino.

As soon as we got out of the launch that had brought us to the beach, I felt an icy wind lashing at me. At every step I took, my heavy rubber boots sank into the mud. I had trouble making headway, weighed down as I was with a knapsack on my back, which bent me double, and burdened with my cameras. I could just barely extract each foot from the peat of the channel banks. We then walked along some wire fencing which Don Faustino had put up to keep the sheep from getting lost in that treacher-

The Beagle Channel

ous countryside—some twenty-eight miles of it. What a job that must have been, given the terrain. Thanks to a very clever system of alternating pastures, he managed to feed some 4,500 sheep on this practically grassless island.

On the other side of the fence was an extraordinary forest. Relatively well protected from the wind, the trees were majestically large. We were walking toward its center, in the semidarkness of thick vegetation. It was necessary to climb over fallen tree trunks, to push our way through branches which lashed at our faces, among enormous roots thrust up through the ground. The forest gave the impression of being a maze, but my guide walked on imperturbably. In the profound silence I heard nothing but the sound of our footsteps. It was a birdless forest. "Yet there are lots of birds in other forests, and especially in the lagoons," said Don Faustino.

We finally emerged from the thick woods into a swampy glade. The air was humid, almost hot. I suddenly had the sensation of being in a tropical region. We arrived at the foot of a very steep slope covered with huge oaks. Then came a real climb. Everything was slippery, and I was soon covered with mud. To the right and left of the steep path, hidden under little green leaves, I found strawberries. They had a delicious taste and were wonderfully refreshing to my dry throat. With the greatest difficulty, I made it up to the plateau. There, in a few minutes, the wind dried the sweat that covered my body. An icy shower after a Turkish bath!

A vast panorama was spread out before me. All around were little undulating islands, partially covered with dense forests and separated from one another by innumerable channels. Picton Island was studded with lagoons. On the north side, far in the background, was the silhouette of the *Micalvi*, anchored in Banner Bay. It looked like a child's toy.

Don Faustino had promised me that I would find the road easy at the top; but there was peat also on the plateau. I was walking into the sun and was blinded by the light. The ground was covered with vegetation and low woody bushes called *chaura* or *calafate*, which bore little red fruits, similar to bilberries, but

Loading bales of wool, Tierra del Fuego

with a more bitter taste. Don Faustino set fire to some weeds. In a few seconds the wind had spread it hundreds of yards. The ashes would regenerate the earth and the smoke would let his wife know he was arriving: in those regions it played the part of a telegraph.

It was not until seven in the evening, in complete darkness, that I saw the outlines of the *estancia*. Big raindrops began to fall when we finally arrived at the low wooden house. Don Faustino's wife kissed me as if she had known me forever. I took off my boots, but not without difficulty. I was stiff all over. Soon everyone was gathered around the traditional *cazuela de ave*, chicken broth with rice. It was warm near the stove, around which my woolen stockings were drying, while outside the storm was beginning to rage.

The next day, around eight in the morning, I woke up with a start. I heard screams, and the whole house seemed in an uproar. Don Faustino's wife burst into my room. She was so upset she could hardly speak. She pointed to the window. I rushed over, and through the fog, dancing on the waves, was the shadow of a ghost ship. It was the *Micalvi*. But no sooner had it appeared than, unable to come any closer, it turned back. Around ten o'clock, surrounded by Don Faustino's whole family, I witnessed a second and equally fruitless attempt. It was not until the next day that the ship succeeded in casting anchor and that a launch was able to bring the members of the crew ashore. The work awaiting them was arduous. Each crossing of

the little boat was a battle with the unleashed elements. The launch had to be loaded with bales of wool, each weighing over four hundred pounds, then carefully guided over to the *Micalvi*, which was anchored between two rocks. The waves were often over fifteen feet high. Don Faustino watched every embarkation with a worried face. The returns on a year's work depended on the skill of the men maneuvering the launch.

While the work progressed, I made a tour of the house. Don Faustino's wife proudly showed me her vegetable garden, where she grew potatoes, cabbages, and greens—inestimable wealth in those parts. I visited the farm, which employed five laborers. The *Micalvi* brought them tobacco. It was now two months since they had run out of cigarettes. Don Faustino's wife talked volubly. It had been such a long time since her last conversation with a stranger! But thanks to the radio, she had kept up on world events.

The captain sent a messenger to tell me to hurry: the weather was so unsettled that he might have to weigh anchor at any moment. Around six in the evening I left my hosts.

On board, the crew were at their stations; the officers shouted orders and the captain paced up and down on the bridge. He had rings under his eyes: no sleep for twenty-four hours. When the last bale was taken on, we weighed anchor and Picton Island soon disappeared into the fog.

My journey was to last several weeks longer. At Navarino Island I did a story on the Yahgan tribes. I then left the *Micalvi* to make my way to the shores of Lake Fagaño, where I filmed a color documentary on the last Indian survivors of the Ona race. Finally, at Ushuaia, I boarded an Argentinean ship that took me back to the banks of the Plata.

Mr. Morrison, the administrator of the Bosis *estancia*, had made me a present of a puma skin. I was delighted at the idea of taking that trophy back to Europe, but I gave it up when I discovered that the tanner in Buenos Aires, no doubt meaning to please me, had adorned the skin with a huge open mouth and glass eyes. Between wooden fangs, painted white, hung a red felt tongue nine inches long!

30

A Controversial Lady: Evita Perón

After my trip to Tierra del Fuego, I proceeded to Chile as assistant to the director Jacques Remy, who was making a film based on a script by Jules Supervielle; later I went on to Peru and Bolivia, and then finally to Brazil and Ecuador. In all those places I did stories that were published by European and American magazines. In 1950 I returned to Argentina, commissioned by a group of newspapers to do a story on General Perón's regime. The public in Europe, as in the United States, was particularly curious about Evita Perón as a personality.

Buenos Aires had changed a great deal—especially the mentality of its inhabitants. Those whom I had known to be nonchalant and carefree were irritated and concerned. A kind of muffled threat hung over the city: there was a law that anyone who dared to criticize publicly a member of the government was to be imprisoned.

The people spoke of Evita Perón with either boundless admiration or violent hatred. It was said that she treated the workers as cordially as she did men in high office: that was how she won the hearts of the people. For the millions of Argentineans of the same humble origins as herself, she was the living symbol of social advancement.

"You're going to have a lot of trouble getting to her," I was told. "She distrusts foreign journalists; they have almost always treated her badly."

"The Señora receives everyone," I was told by the Minister of Information, Raoul Apold, "but one must be patient." After some time he informed me that the appointment had been arranged. "Next Friday, at the Ministry of Labor. Bring your camera, and above all, eat something before you come. The appointment is for 6 P.M., but the Señora works late."

A few minutes before six, I climbed the stairs that led to Evita's reception room. I was taken to an office where other people were already waiting. On one wall were large photographs of Evita and the General, separated by a crucifix.

Two elderly gentlemen were settled on a sofa. A young woman with a huge bouquet of flowers was sitting shyly on the edge of a chair. A fat Egyptian had sunk into an armchair. Four tradesmen from Rosario stood talking in undertones. Evita had procured the sum necessary for them to start what was now a prospering business. They had come to thank her and to bring her gifts: a refrigerator and a large rug with the name "Evita" embroidered on it. The gifts were waiting in front of the door.

By the large clock it was seven-thirty, then eight, then eight-thirty. From time to time other people were shown in. The tiny room was packed. Nine o'clock. Everyone was becoming edgy. Ten o'clock. My legs were growing numb: the air had become unbreathable. The one ashtray was overflowing with cigarette butts.

"I've been here since four this afternoon," muttered the young woman, whose large bouquet of flowers had wilted. She looked unhappy. From time to time the sound of numerous voices could be heard through the closed door; a loudspeaker blared out the Peronist anthem, and then once again there was silence.

At midnight the affable secretary reappeared: "The Señora has gone to a meeting of the butchers' union. All of you come back in a week."

The following Friday there we all were, back in the same office, worried about the very same thing: How long would we have to wait? But this time we waited only a little under three hours. A guard showed us into a large hall furnished, like a people's theatre, with wooden benches one next to the other; they were occupied by poorly dressed women and children. Babies cried and uniformed guards brought them bottles. Small groups of people stood all along the walls: workers' delegations. Two photographers, with cameras in hand, waited in a corner. The immense hall was filled with cigarette smoke. And there, facing that mixed assemblage, sitting behind an enormous desk, and surrounded by about a half-dozen secretaries, I caught sight of a pale young woman: Evita Perón.

In that atmosphere of a smoky waiting room, in the midst of all those wretched onlookers, she seemed like a magical apparition, an angel come down from heaven. Her extraordinary white skin emphasized her huge eyes. Her platinum-blond hair was half hidden under a little hat. She was wearing a dark suit, perfectly cut. "It's a Christian Dior," my neighbor, the fat Egyptian, whispered to me admiringly. Pinned on the young woman's chest was a huge brooch made of brilliants and blue sapphires in the shape and colors of the national flag. Her long pale hands played with a pencil. Her red nails were carefully polished. Rings set with precious stones and diamonds covered her fingers. She gave the impression of being extremely fragile.

The people sitting in front of her—mothers of large families accompanied by their children, workers with hands deformed by their labor, office workers, shop assistants, clerks, slum dwellers—all were gaping at her. I myself was fascinated, but mostly by the contrast.

"The Señora dispenses charity and works miracles every Friday afternoon," one of the guards told me. "It's impossible for her to refuse anything to the poor."

"Do these poor people all belong to the Peronist movement?"

"Of course, otherwise the Señora wouldn't help them."

Evita was a fairy, beyond any doubt, but a political fairy. She suddenly rose and made her way through the crowd, shaking

Waiting for Evita Perón

hands with everyone she happened to pass. With me as well. It was a damp, feverish hand.

"All of you come along with me, *muchachos,*" she said, as she disappeared into a large amphitheatre. It was already full, and the streamers decorating the rostrum indicated that the people there belonged to the film workers' union. As soon as Evita appeared, the crowd began to chant frantically: "Evita! Evita!" while a phonograph blared out the Peronist anthem. Photographers and film makers sat at the foot of the rostrum. A union representative handed her a check made out to her organization, "Social Assistance." Evita thanked him in a three-minute speech. Then the Peronist anthem was played again, and Evita withdrew. The whole ceremony lasted no more than six minutes, but the people gathered there had waited for hours.

She had that kind of reception several times a day. However, those "voluntary" donations of workers' groups were not as voluntary and spontaneous as one might have thought: Evita procured raises in salaries for the workers, but it was the rule that they hand over the first month's raise to her for her charitable works. When unions with hundreds of thousands of members were involved, the check sometimes ran into the millions. Evita used the money as she saw fit. No one ever asked her for an accounting.

When I returned to her office, I found the door closed. "You can't go in now," said a guard. "Come back some other day." Evita had left for a propaganda tour of the provinces.

It was not until a month later that I saw her again in her office. She was talking to a young man who was explaining to her that he had just been married and that his house was occupied by some other family. He asked Evita to help him put them out.

"How many of you are there?"

"Four people."

"And how many people are in the family now occupying your house?"

"Eight."

"Then," replied Evita, "continue living with your parents.

The other family needs the house more than you do."

The young man protested:

"But it's my own house. That's an injustice!"

"I'm the one who decides what's just and unjust," interrupted Evita. With the flick of an eyelid, she signaled two guards, who took the young man away, struggling. Silence prevailed.

"What are they going to do with him?"

"They're simply taking him to jail. That's 'justicialism,' " a secretary told me. "The Señora settled the question."

The crowd kept growing. The women and children summoned by Social Assistance had disappeared. Now there were only men in the room. All union delegates. They had come to discuss labor problems with Evita. She settled, decided, promised. It was almost always a question of raises in salary. Evita agreed every time, and the delegates went away beaming.

One of the secretaries, deep in a chair at the back of the room, was wiping his brow.

"This place is a *manicomio* [madhouse]," he told me. "It's like this every day."

It was not until around two in the morning that I managed to exchange a few words with Evita.

"Take all the photographs you want here," she told me with a smile. "I have no private life. You must have realized that."

I did, and I photographed her talking with a workers' delegation. Then Evita insisted on being photographed with me by her personal photographer. It was her way of rewarding a visitor.

A few days later the Minister of Information telephoned me: "This evening you are to go to the Presidential residence to photograph the Señora in her gala dress, before she leaves for the Independence Day celebration at the Colon Theatre."

Evita had probably liked my photographs.

For the first time, I climbed the steps to the Presidential residence, on the Avenida Alvear. I was shown into a spacious drawing room, decorated with a large tapestry.

Evita appeared, accompanied by the General. She introduced me to her husband, who smiled amiably. Perón was tall and slim, elegant in his dress uniform. But his red face was covered with acne.

Evita was wearing a sky-blue tulle dress, studded with pearls, and was wrapped in an ostrich-feather cape.

"This dress was designed for me by Christian Dior."

Her hair was drawn back into curls at the nape of her neck, and she was wearing a three-strand pearl necklace. Her rings and pendant earrings came from Van Cleef and Arpels.

While a dressmaker finished arranging the pleats of her skirt, the General waited patiently.

"My decorations," Evita told her personal maid, who began to pin a brochette of them onto her chest.

"You see, Madame, I also have the Legion of Honor," Evita pointed out to me.

The General looked at his wife with a critical eye. On his mouth was the hint of a mischievous and paternal smile. "Your opponents will again say you look like a *bataclana* [chorus girl]." But Evita was too absorbed to hear him.

Evita Perón

190   The next day a secretary escorted me directly to Evita's
private suite on the second floor of the residence. She was sitting
in the entrance hall, from which one could look straight down
into the large drawing room. She was being combed out by her
hairdresser and having her nails done by a manicurist, while her
private secretary set up her schedule for the day and took notes.
Just a few steps away several men carrying heavy leather brief-
cases waited patiently. They were all government ministers,
who, before meeting with the Head of State, never failed to pay
a visit to Evita. It was eight in the morning, but the drawing
room downstairs was already beginning to fill up. As the groom-
ing process came to an end, she talked matters over with the
ministers. It must have been somewhat like the way Madame de
Pompadour began her day, except that Evita seemed to make all
the decisions herself.

"I would like to see your dresses, Señora. I've heard so
much about them."

I knew that clothes were her weakness. She immediately
took me into a large room lined with closets.

"Here I keep only my evening gowns. They all come from
Paris," she noted. A maid helped her take some of them out.

Dozens of dresses filed past my eyes and my camera; then
came the fur coats. In another room, nothing but hats: I counted
more than a hundred of them. Evita posed willingly and tried on
a hat. Then there was the room reserved for shoes. Evita Peron
was no longer the austere public figure settling social conflicts;
I could see that she took a very feminine pleasure in showing
another woman clothes that would be the envy of any queen.

To crown the morning I was allowed to peer into the five-
level safe that contained her jewels. Brilliants and precious
stones proclaimed their worth. It was a collection worthy of
Cleopatra.

"All these jewels are gifts," she confided to me in a voice
filled with emotion. And it was true. Everyone knew her weakness, and those who asked favors of her never forgot it. Evita in
no way hid her taste for jewels. She visited the poorest neighborhoods stunningly dressed and dispensed charity wearing pre-

Preparing for a gala

cious stones worth thousands. In fact, that was one of the things that enchanted her devotees.

"Evita used to be like us," they would say, "and look at her now. It shows that we can all get the same thing . . ."

For them she personified a marvelous dream come true.

Evita was about to make a tour of her charitable institutions, and she took me along.

"I would like you to leave with a fair idea of the institutions I've created; we're going to visit a rest home for the poor."

The powerful car stopped in front of a modern building.

Evita no sooner looked around than she was beside herself.

"Where is the directress?" she shouted. "Who gave orders to cover the carpet and put slipcovers on the furniture in the entrance hall? Didn't I have you informed that I was arriving this morning with a photographer who takes color photographs? It's incredible; you're all dismissed." They were all nuns and looked crestfallen.

"You have no idea how beautiful all this furniture is! All of it is covered in red velvet, and," lifting up the slipcover of an armchair, "look how comfortable and modern it is; haven't the poor the right to live like the rich, at least for a few days?"

In that same spirit she had sent off three hundred of the poorest children to spend a two-week holiday in one of the largest luxury hotels in Mar del Plata, the Argentinean Deauville, only to send them back afterward to their wretched lodgings. It was her way of making social reforms.

The inside of the rest home, which was intended as a shelter for the unemployed, looked as if it had been decorated for a movie star. The people in residence at the time were shyly sitting on the edges of their chairs. When Evita showed me the bedrooms, I had the impression that no one lived in them. Their temporary occupants were not allowed to stay there during the day so that everything would remain in place, for the Señora often arrived unexpectedly with prominent visitors.

The next day I arrived at the General San Martin Restaurant on the Avenida de Mayo, where Evita had invited me to lunch. It was four in the afternoon. She was surrounded by some half-dozen ministers.

Evita Perón

The Minister of the Interior was speaking. "But Señora, you should not have signed that decree!"

"It's just another signature. What difference does it make?" Evita interrupted. Then she asked them as a group: "What will be done with the five million? Which of you wants it for his ministry?"

The ministers impressed me as a bunch of schoolboys, altogether dominated by her will. No doubt about it: she was the one who gave the orders. Few women in history have ever wielded such power. She was only thirty-two.

The next day I brought some thirty prints to her at the residence. Evita was delighted.

"Let the whole world see what I own," she cried.

The Minister of Information did not seem to be of the same opinion. At midnight he telephoned me: "Tomorrow morning I shall be waiting for you at the ministry. Have all the negatives with you. This is an order!" His voice was harsh. I promised, but at seven in the morning I left by plane with all my photographs.

When my story on Evita was published in *Life* magazine and in newspapers throughout the world, it provoked a diplomatic incident. In Argentina *Life* was put on the blacklist. In all the texts accompanying my photographs, Evita's taste in clothes and jewels had been ridiculed.

Even if her methods of improving conditions for the working classes left something to be desired, Peronism had generated great hope among the workers.

31

Mexico
and Diego Rivera

When the writer Alfonso Reyes invited me to give a lecture at the Colegio de Mexico, I planned to spend a few weeks there. I stayed for two years.

"Mexico," said one of its writers, "is like a tramp in rags who makes so bold as to wear a tie with a gold stickpin." He was thinking of the skyscrapers, the large boulevards lined with Cadillacs, the ultramodern hotels of the capital, in such sharp contrast to the houses of dried mud that serve as lodgings for the poor Mexican peasants.

During those two years I crossed the country, which is almost as large as Europe, from one end to the other. I visited Yucatán in the tropics, where the temples and Mayan palaces are decorated with hieroglyphics that no scholar has yet been able to decipher. I did a story on the women of the Isthmus of Tehuantepec, who are reputed to be the most beautiful in Mexico. I went to Lake Pátzcuaro on All Souls' Day, when the village people gather at night in the cemetery, with offerings. I paid a visit to the Tetzotl Indians, who live on the Guatemalan border, in Sierra Madre, speak a language of their own, and have their own government. I attended innumerable fiestas, which per-

195

Alfonso Reyes, 1952

Mexican peasant

At Lake Pátzcuaro

petuate the traditions of an extraordinarily vital and colorful folklore. The dancers often wear costumes and masks, and are accompanied by musicians who play languorous melodies punctuated by the explosion of firecrackers.

What fascinated me most of all was the art—not only the pre-Columbian art but also the modern art, which can be found on the walls of most of the public buildings. Stimulated by the ideas of the revolution, in which they had taken an active part, the painters wanted to paint "for the people." They considered that easel-painting was meant for connoisseurs and had to be replaced by large murals and frescoes in all public places, so as to bring joy to the entire population. The liberal governments gave them the means to carry out their plans for social art. In the years following the revolution of 1921, and under the direction of three great artists—Diego Rivera, José Clemente Orozco, and David Alfaro Siqueiros—a new genre of monumental painting developed in Mexico, patterned after the pre-Columbian bas-reliefs and the murals of the colonial period.

Diego Rivera was the most popular, for his realistic style was accessible to the masses. I met him as soon as I arrived. At the age of sixty-eight he weighed over 200 pounds and seemed gifted with extraordinary physical strength and almost superhuman endurance. I often saw him painting in a public building, perched on the scaffolding like a ponderous eagle. He told me that he got up every morning at six. An hour later he was already at work and did not stop until midnight.

One day I visited him in his studio at San Angel, a suburb of Mexico City. He had just begun a canvas portraying a little girl.

"It's lovely," I said when he had finished. "I would like to buy it."

"Fine. Ten thousand pesos."

I was dismayed. With that much money I could live in Mexico for a year!

"How can you charge me such a price! It didn't take you more than an hour."

"So that it would take me one hour, I have worked sixty years," he replied pensively.

Diego was right, and I had to make do with photographing the canvas.

When the painter was at work, he concentrated passionately, completely sincere and dedicated. But when he stopped painting, his overflowing energy would drive him to do unpredictable things. A fantastic liar, he created numerous scandals. He was a great puzzle to the government, for he was forever advertising his political choices by incorporating Marxist slogans into his monumental frescoes, one of the reasons why foreigners wrongly conclude that Mexico is a revolutionary country. Diego's personal fame was greater then that of most film stars. When he ambled into a restaurant, his large, potbellied figure encased in a flapping jacket, and his protruding eyes gazing mournfully upon the world, he would always attract tourists wanting to snap his picture. Like the beaches of Acapulco, the floating gardens of Xochimilco, and the jewelry of Monte Alban, he represented one of the country's chief tourist attractions, and so the government allowed him to paint his frescoes as he saw fit.

Never was an artist as honored by the state during his lifetime as Diego Rivera. In 1949 the whole Palace of Fine Arts was devoted to a gigantic exhibit, celebrating the painter's works produced over a period of fifty years. Riveras were sent there from all over the world. The exhibit was shown for several months and was visited by more than a million people.

Rivera was one of the first members of the Mexican Communist Party, founded in 1921. But because of his anarchic turn of mind, he was ousted a few years later for lack of discipline. He then flirted with the Fourth International and obtained from the government a resident's visa for Leon Trotsky. When Trotsky was assassinated in 1940, Diego publicly accused Stalin's agents, but a few years later he wanted to join the Communist Party again and humbly acknowledged his "criminal offenses." Once he was readmitted, the first act of that very contradictory character was to have his grandson baptized in the Catholic church and to choose as godmother a Mexican movie star: Maria Felix.

He was married three times. His first marriage, in Paris, was to Angelina Beloff, a Russian painter. They divorced a few years later but remained good friends. His second marriage, to Guadaloupe Marin, a woman of great beauty and violent temperament, and the mother of his two daughters, also ended in divorce. They too remained good friends. Finally, in 1928, when he was forty-two, he married Frida Kahlo, an eighteen-year-old painter. Then began the tragic period in Diego's life.

Frida had been injured in an automobile accident the year before. When she met the artist, she was still walking on crutches but seemed on the road to recovery. Actually, her spinal column had been affected. From the time of their marriage to her death in 1954, Frida had to undergo twenty-two operations; during the last of them one of her legs was amputated. A heroic, almost legendary figure, confined to her wheelchair year after year, she sat at her easel painting terrifying pictures in the surrealist manner. Strangely beautiful, she had a quick mind and biting wit. She and Diego constantly quarreled, but she understood him better than anyone else, and they could not live without each other. She divorced him all the same, but at the end of a year they remarrried. "Diego is like a child," she would say. "Now that we're older, perhaps we shall find peace together."

The painter invited me to go with him to San Pablo Tepetlapa, a small village sitting in the middle of a bleak lava plain, bristling with prickly plants. There, in great secrecy, he was building a pyramid patterned after those of the Mayas and Aztecs.

"It's here that I want to store my ten-thousand-piece collection of pre-Columbian art," he told me, "as well as my ashes and Frida's."

It was a huge building, several floors high. Inside, in the semidarkness, were many recesses to house his treasures. The ceilings were decorated with mosaics, designed by the painter in pre-Columbian style.

When Diego died in 1959, the man who did not believe in God, but had built a temple, was buried according to the rites of the Catholic church. The government was opposed to his urn

Frida Kahlo, 1952

being entombed in his temple; it did, however, become a museum, as he had wished.

When I wanted to leave Mexico for the United States, I had some trouble with the American consulate—it was the era of McCarthyism. The profession of photo-reporter, of course, involves certain risks. Because of my frequent visits to Diego Rivera, I had probably been denounced. Yet my story on his temple was published by *Look*—a magazine that could hardly be called leftist. Indeed, *Look* devoted several pages to the painter. As an artist, Rivera was admired throughout the world, and Mexico still considers him one of its greatest painters. As a politican, no one, not even his own government—however much he defied it —took him seriously.

Diego Rivera, with his mural, "The Creation of the World," 1952

modern life has made it necessary to reduce information to its essentials. No one has time any more to read newspapers every day from beginning to end; most people skim through them, and many merely read the headlines. On the other hand, by absorbing a series of pictures at a glance, we are quickly informed about the main events of the week. It is easier to remember a concrete image than to retain ideas expressed in language. The texts that point up such photographs are generally very brief, and if the series of images is properly conceived, it constitutes a perfectly clear language.

The popularity of this new type of journalism, based almost exclusively on pictures, is due largely to modern man's change in status and to a tendency to greater and greater standardization. The individual as such becomes insignificant, but his moral need to assert himself as an individual increases. The huge success of war correspondent Ernie Pyle lay in the fact that, in his stories about the front, rather than describing the lives of the GIs in general, he told about what had happened to Bob Smith of Brownsville, Texas, or Jim Brown of Nashville, Tennessee. Millions of American readers thus had the moral satisfaction of being able to identify the fates of their own brothers, husbands, or sons with the lives of the GIs described by Pyle. The success of the illustrated weeklies is based on the same phenomenon. Apart from news events, they tell stories that are relevant to the lives of the mass of readers, but always with specific names attached to the persons involved. As the actual relationships between men become increasingly dehumanized, the journalist tends to give the individual an artificial importance.

Most picture-magazine covers portray a celebrity—that is, the face of some well-known personality, some big name: a movie star, an actress, a popular singer, an athlete, a royal couple, even a head of state. But to help the cause, pseudo-celebrities may also be created. Indeed, they have one advantage: they correspond perfectly to the yearnings of the masses. Thus someone who was completely unknown yesterday may become famous tomorrow if his photograph appears on the front page of a big newspaper or on the cover of a mass-circulation magazine.

George Bernard Shaw

James Joyce

Virginia Woolf

Victoria Sackville-West

H. G. Wells

Henry Miller

Jean-Paul Sartre and Simone de Beauvoir

Katherine Anne Porter

In the fall of 1953 *Weekend Picture Magazine,* the Sunday supplement of a whole chain of Canadian newspapers with a circulation of several million, proposed to do a story on the Royal Canadian Air Force stationed in Germany.

In Canada military service is not compulsory. To encourage young men and women to join the armed forces at that time, posters were put up everywhere identifying military service with traveling for pleasure: "Join the army and see the world."

Weekend Picture Magazine rushed one of its best journalists to Europe to write the article; I was commissioned to take the photographs.

As soon as we arrived at Zweibrücken, in Germany, where the R.C.A.F. was based, the journalist advised me to visit the girls' building.

"Look at them carefully and choose the one most representative of the ideal Canadian girl—one of our nice girls with whom parents can identify their daughter, or brothers their sister. . . ."

The young lady I thought best corresponded to those demands was called Sonia Nichols. Simple, smiling, photogenic, she had blond hair and blue eyes. She thus became the heroine of the story that appeared in *Weekend Picture Magazine* a few weeks later, entitled "Airwomen Overseas."

The journalist told how twenty-year-old Sonia, born in Berwick, Nova Scotia, had never had the opportunity to leave home until she joined the R.C.A.F. But since she had been in the armed forces, she had seen a good deal of her own country, traveled in Germany, and visited Paris and Switzerland; before the end of her overseas assignment, she would probably also get to Italy and Scandinavia. At the airbase she was learning foreign languages, visiting German families in the area, and going out with friends on sightseeing tours. She got her exercise in an ultramodern gym and in a fine swimming pool. In short, thanks to her job in the armed forces, Sonia's life had become fascinating and full of experiences she never would have had otherwise.

Several pages of my photographs illustrated the text: Sonia holding the baby of "Frau Else Gratz . . . at home," drinking

34

Apology for an Error: Nabokov

The work of a photographer does not end with the development of his photographs: he must edit them as well. It is of great importance that they be captioned very carefully; an inexact or incorrect description may have troublesome consequences.

A book published by UNESCO included one of my photographs of a Mexican temple. Some time later an indignant letter arrived from a reader who lived over six thousand miles from Mexico. He complained that an error had been made in the name of the monument. He was right: the publisher had to add an erratum slip.

In 1965 my book *James Joyce in Paris, His Final Years,* consisting of my photographs of the writer, pictures of Paris in the 1930s, and portraits of men of letters of that period, came out in New York, and in it I had made another mistake. The volume contained a photograph of the readers' committee of the review *Mesures,* composed of several literary personalities, including Jean Paulhan, Michel Leiris, Henri Michaux, and someone whom I seemed to recognize as the playright Jacques Audiberti. The *Figaro Littéraire* published it when the book came out and used the names I had furnished. Jean Paulhan promptly sent a

(From left to right) *Sylvia Beach, Barbara Church, Vladimir Nabokov, Adrienne Monnier, Germaine Paulhan, Henry Church, Henri Michaux, Michel Leiris and* (behind him) *Jean Paulhan. The editorial board of* **Mesures**, *at Henry Church's villa in Ville d'Avray, April 1937*

note to the editorial staff, pointing out that I was in error. The man I had called Audiberti was none other than Vladimir Nabokov, father of *Lolita*.

"The writer standing behind Barbara Church [her husband was the American partner in *Mesures*] is Nabokov, an admirable writer, who had just contributed a story 'Mademoiselle O,' to *Mesures*, and at the same time, a study on Pushkin to *La Nouvelle Revue Française*. . . ."

I at once sent a note of apology to Nabokov, and when I visited Switzerland a few weeks later to do a story, I decided to go and see him to apologize in person and to photograph him again.

He and his wife live in a hotel in Montreux, where they generally spend the winter months. He immediately began to read me the preface to his latest book, *Speak, Memory*, in which he mentioned my mistake, showing that he must have been very struck by the fact that I had neglected to associate him with the literary movement in France during the 1930s.

Nabokov told me that he remembered the day perfectly and that he had taken a taxi to the Churches' in Ville d'Avray, along with Adrienne Monnier, Sylvia Beach, and one other person he could no longer recall.

"I, my dear Nabokov," I replied, "was also in a taxi with Adrienne Monnier, Sylvia Beach, and one other person I could no longer recall."

Vladimir Nabokov, 1967

36

Some French Writers and an American Gentleman

When I again settled down in Paris in the fifties, a new generation of writers and artists had come to the fore. Jean-Paul Sartre and Albert Camus dominated the postwar literary scene in France. In painting, Picasso, Matisse, Bonnard, Braque, and Chagall were still the undisputed masters, and of the younger group the painter Jean Dubuffet and the sculptor Alberto Giacometti were coming into prominence.

Besides existentialist literature, with Sartre as its foremost exponent, various movements were springing up, among them the "Lettrists," led by Isidore Isou, and the "new novelists," with Nathalie Sarraute, Claude Simon, Robert Pinget, Alain Robbe-Grillet, and Michel Butor. In theatre the new plays were signed Samuel Beckett and Eugène Ionesco.

Many foreign writers and artists had again chosen to live in Paris. The Lost Generation of the twenties had been replaced by a whole new wave of Americans, many of whom were former GIs, like Irwin Shaw, who preferred to settle in Paris than be harassed by witch-hunting committees, or Richard Wright, who was escaping from racism.

I had met Wright in 1947, and when I visited Buenos Aires in 1950 to do my story on Evita Perón, his *Native Son* was being

filmed there, with him in the leading role. We became friends, 227
and I went almost daily to watch the film being made. It was an
Argentinean production. One day, on the set, I heard a technician shout: "The Negro can just wait." I realized that racism
existed even in that country, where there were no blacks. Luckily, Richard Wright did not understand Spanish. I knew that as
a child in the South he had been traumatized by racism, which
he has described in *Uncle Tom's Children*. Paris for him meant
freedom: there, he was accepted everywhere.

Paul Celan, nowadays considered the greatest poet in German of our time, had also preferred to live in Paris, where he
committed suicide in 1970. Among the South Americans were
the Argentinean writer Julio Cortazar, the Chilean painter
Sebastian Matta, and many others.

Indeed, Paris had again become one of the intellectual and
artistic centers where controversial opinions were passionately
expressed and new ideas generated. I photographed most of
those artists and writers, but I also took new photos of those I
had known before the war and who were now famous, such as
the poet Henri Michaux and Jean-Paul Sartre.

Very few photographs of Michaux exist. I believe that only
Brassaï and I had the good fortune to photograph him.

"Why do you always refuse to pose?" I asked him.

"Anyone who wants to see me has only to read me. My true
face is in my books."

His answer implied a preference for showing the public
only the image that the poet created, rather than a physical
appearance recorded by the camera. He was probably right. Yet
when we finish a book that has moved us, we wonder about the
writer's face, about the eyes that have discovered unexplored
regions; we thirst to know the form that imprisons such talent.

Sartre, on the other hand, is very indulgent when it comes
to cameras. He knows that he is not handsome, and he doesn't
care. In his company one is immediately fascinated by his intelligence and charmed by his voice. His whole personality exudes
a human warmth that puts his listener at ease.

Making contact with Simone de Beauvoir is more difficult.
She is extremely reserved. It was in Adrienne Monnier's book-

Saint-John Perse, 1966

Richard Wright, 1959

shop that I first met her. She was a handsome girl with regular features.

One morning in December 1954 I received a telephone call from the head of publicity for the publishing house Gallimard. A touch of anguish could be discerned in his generally cheerful voice.

"Something dreadful has happened."

"What?" I cried out, imagining the worst.

"We've just been tipped off that Simone de Beauvoir is getting the Prix Goncourt today, and she has disappeared!"

I knew Simone and was not at all surprised. She fled from publicity and photographers, and had a horror of the cheap tabloids that pry into people's private lives. She and Sartre had often been unpleasantly publicized. They had been reproached for their leftist ideas, and she, above all, had been criticized for her refusal to legalize their relationship. The bourgeoisie never forgave her for trampling on their most sacred principles. In literary circles some claimed that she never would have gained renown had she not been Sartre's companion. On the other hand, the Prix Goncourt had been created to help young writers, just starting out, whereas it was clear that in the case of Simone de Beauvoir's *Les Mandarins,* it was being awarded to the work of a writer in the prime of life; that might have troubled Simone. But I also knew that the winner's disappearance would have driven any press agent crazy!

In a few hours the jury's annual luncheon was to take place, followed by the official announcement of the winner's name. It would be the most important news of the day. Journalists and photographers were no doubt already on the scene at the Drouant restaurant.

Now where on earth was Simone? Surely not at home, and not at Sartre's either. Suddenly I had an inspiration. A few minutes later I was at the door of her mother's home on the rue Blomet. And it was there that I took a series of photographs of a very surprised Simone.

"If it has to be done," she said, "you're the one I have most confidence in. The *Paris Match* photographers keep watch on my house night and day, but they don't know that it has two exits.

Jean-Paul Sartre and Simone de Beauvoir

Jean-Paul Sartre, 1965

Jean-Paul Sartre, 1969

Simone de Beauvoir

Tennessee Williams, 1964

nized John Steinbeck in the crowd, busy signing traveler's checks. It was dark inside, which is why, in my picture, he appears against a dark background that recalls the effect of Rembrandt's chiaroscuro.

Henry Miller and I got on immediately. He simply came up to my studio, where I photographed him on my terrace against the pale blue Paris sky he loved so well and which brought back to him so many memories. "Being famous," he said, "can be an awful burden. But I always agree to receive journalists and photographers, for I have never forgotten my own difficult years, when I too was one of them." There was a great man who understood our problems.

I visited Mary McCarthy in Paris on assignment. *The New York Times* had asked me to photograph her in order to illustrate the review of her novel *The Group*. I found her a tall, slender woman with a sophisticated look in her eyes, sparkling with wit, and not always charitable to others. She was decorating her new rue de Rennes apartment. Her bedroom windows looked out onto a lovely, hidden convent garden. One might have been out in the country. When my picture appeared in the paper and on the jacket of her novel, no one would have thought it had been taken in the heart of Paris.

Thanks to Mary, I met the distinguished and shy poet Robert Lowell, whom I photographed on a café terrace near the Madeleine.

James Jones belongs to that group of American writers who have chosen to live on the Ile Saint-Louis. He bought an eighteenth-century house, remodeled it to his taste, and filled it with his collection of paintings by American artists. I had to admire his bedroom, with its carpeting, covering not only the floor but the ceiling and walls as well. The bathroom, entirely of marble, might have belonged to a great Hollywood star. From his studio one could see the spires of Notre-Dame and the charming quays of the Seine. How wonderful to be a best-selling author!

In the fall of 1970 I visited Katherine Anne Porter. She too belongs to the happy few who became best sellers. She lives at College Park, a university town between Baltimore and Washington. I admire her meticulous, disciplined, classic style. Her short stories are gems. I had read "Flowering Judas" when the French translation of it came out in *Mesures* in 1936. Our paths had crossed several times without our ever having actually met. She too had been present at T. S. Eliot's reading in Sylvia Beach's bookshop, Shakespeare and Company.

When I recall her, a curious thing happens, particularly for a photographer. Instead of a small lady with very fine features on which the years have taken their toll, I see a beautiful young woman with enormous eyes that seem to look at a world visible only to herself. This is the picture that for so many years I had seen on the wall of Shakespeare and Company. Her lively personality, her lucid brain, her flow of eloquence, her caustic wit, all have contributed to producing this very personal image.

When I fractured my ankle crossing a street in New York, I had to postpone the appointment I had made to visit her. "The list of broken bones among persons I know grows like an endemic malediction," wrote Katherine Anne Porter to me when she heard of the accident. "My friend and agent broke her ankle stepping off a curb in New York. I fractured my left hip. A helpful friend at the University fractured three ribs. My nurse fractured her left wrist and you, oh dear! fractured your ankle!

"Alas, only time can heal us. Do you know that you have not

Robert Lowell, 1963

only my sympathetic thoughts as for all suffering creatures, but an immediate intense very personal fellowship in the feel of broken bones."

When finally I arrived at her apartment, I heard that her fractured hip had been preceded by a badly wrenched shoulder and an injured knee, three accidents that had taken place in the last five months.

"I have not been able to work for a year; constant pain, anxiety, and frustration; what have I done to deserve a year like that?"

But her courage was high. We talked of many things, particularly of Katherine Anne Porter.

I looked around. The charming apartment was exquisitely decorated. In her spacious dining room she had set up a small

Mary McCarthy, 1964

fountain surrounded by greenery; water trickled in a continuous cascade. There was old Italian furniture, a large mahogany table, comfortable chairs. We walked through her study, lined with books and papers. A large basket was filled with letters.

"All this must be answered," she said with a sigh. We entered her bedroom.

"I spend most of my time in bed, where I do most of my living. I read a lot. Ever since I was a small child, I have read all the time. My family were insatiable readers; there were books everywhere in our house. When I was about fourteen, my father took me over to the books and said 'Start here.' It was a collection of volumes, each as big as a telephone directory. I deciphered their titles: The Philosphical Dictionary of Voltaire, with notes by Tobias Smollett. I started with them. We bought the Henry James books as they came out. He died in 1916, and I had all his works. One time later somebody came and said, 'but you've got a fortune. I bet you never thought of it.' I asked, 'What is it?' 'You have a first edition of Henry James!' 'But darling,' I said, 'there was never any other.' He is my love and my ideal. But now he has become terribly controversial; there is a whole school against him, and when someone wants to bring me down, they say: 'under the influence of Henry James.' When they want to praise me, they say: 'under the influence of James Joyce.' I wish they would just leave me alone. I did not expect all that happened to me. I did not ask for it and I have not enjoyed it much."

Later, I looked at the frail lady before me in her beautiful Dior nightgown, resting in her Venetian bed. Through the window, through the mist, one could see the trees and their leaves colored by the fall, flamboyant red, speckled brown. But for Katherine Anne Porter it was already winter. Her long life had been filled with torment and hardships. Fame came late to her. She was seventy-two when her first and only novel, *Ship of Fools* became a best seller. It brought her over a million dollars. A collection of her essays and occasional writings appeared in April 1970 in only one volume.

"Someone rebuked me for not writing more or publishing

John Steinbeck, 1961

more," she said. " 'Well, I remember the thousands of letters I have written since the age of eighteen,' I answered; and he said: 'I know, you have written in letters the equivalent of fifty books.' I have also talked them away," she added laughing. "And then I was married. Believe me, it's perfect madness for a woman who is an artist to marry and not give all her time to her work. To be a writer is not a part-time job, and thinking one can marry and run a house and have children and keep up social life, which you have to do if you have a husband . . . it's madness. I have seen too many women try it; it's a disaster, or leads to divorce, or one is ruined as an artist and has to give up."

"But you married three times?"

"Yes, I did it because I was crazy in love with those creatures. I am a very affectionate woman and live on love and have to have it, but love takes so many forms. The fact that you have a heart does not mean that you have a brain. I hope and pray I have both, a poet's heart to love with."

"When did you first marry?"

"I eloped in New Orleans when I was sixteen, but I said I was eighteen, because the law stipulated that a girl can't get married without her parents' consent under eighteen. It may still be so. My husband was twenty-one, and both families, when they learned about it, were furious. They were not at all happy about this marriage, and on top of everything it had not taken place in church with a priest, only before the judge. We were both Catholic and that is the way we were raised. My husband's family was very rich: cotton, coffee, corn, sugar . . . they bought the crop and sold it. I came from a family who had lost everything in the Civil War except land. We were what is called in the South 'land poor.' Very soon I realized that my marriage was a disaster; I was utterly wretched. I wrote my father that I wanted to come home, that I was terribly sorry. But he acted the heavy father; he turned it into a melodrama and wrote just one line: 'You have made your bed, now lie in it.' You know, in those days it was such a scandalous thing to get a divorce and even leave your husband. My marriage was unbearable, but divorce for mental cruelty did not exist then. We stayed married nearly seven years.

"From the time I was six, I had been trying to write. I tried to write in different styles for practice, and my husband quarreled all the time about my writing; he even got angry seeing me writing a letter. Henry James spent twenty years trying to write and he probably worked much harder than I ever did, but my husband when he saw the exercises tried to take them away from me and destroy them. What an incredible fool I was!"

"In spite of this experience you married again?"

"Yes, I did. Twice I married again and each time my husbands got progressively younger, and they made me as unhappy as the first, each in his own different way."

"You lived many years in Mexico, Katherine Anne; many of your short stories have Mexico as a background, but you also spent several years in Paris. Did you like it there?"

"I was so happy in Paris, never mind my bad marriage, the second one, which was beginning to collapse. In spite of the various kinds of hardship I had, I loved it there for one reason above all; Paris is a town where one can be happy without knowing anybody. I opened my eyes in the morning and looked out; no matter how bad the weather was, I felt lovely and renewed again. I was terribly busy. I went everywhere, but I also spent many months at the Cordon Bleu; I wanted to learn to cook. I learned to make spaghetti in Greenwich Village and fried eggs and such kind of things, but you can't live on spaghetti forever. I still have the little iron pots in which I carried home the food I had cooked. When I went home on the bus, I put my project under the seat and when anyone sat down next to me, I would say: 'Please be careful, don't you see, s'il vous plaît, I've my project!' Then I would take the top off it. They would sniff and say 'Hmmm,' kindly.

"At the same time I studied music with a blind man. In my youth I wanted to play the violin, but my grandmother, who brought me up, would not let me. She thought it not appropriate for a lady. But every winter we went from San Antonio to New Orleans to go to the opera and hear concerts. I saw Sarah Bernhardt, I heard Paderewski and all the great musicians, actors, and actresses who came there. Literature and music, that was the kind of family I grew up with. Well, in Paris there was my music, and there was my cooking school and there was my garden. I had a little garden about twice the size of my living room. We lived in 70 bis, rue Notre-Dame-des-Champs. Ezra Pound had lived there before us. I would go around the corner to the Luxembourg and watch the gardeners, and whatever they were planting I would plant, in a miniature way. What pleased me so much were the espalier pears, they called them President Pears, and they tied them up in little paper sacks so that the birds couldn't peck at them."

"Did you meet many French writers?"

"Well, I met them casually in Sylvia Beach's or in Adrienne Monnier's bookshop. With Adrienne I always talked about food. She liked it and I like it. I come from a part of the country that really had good food, but much of the country has appalling food. At home, the Southerners know good food. In the country they had a big smokehouse and they made their own bacon and own hams. We raised our own cattle and had all kinds of beef, and when the game season came we had duck and deer. They had big ovens, you know, and a big square pan that just fitted, and the cook used to make a pie of either pigeon or doves. She roasted them just a little bit first, and quite often she stuffed each one and then put a baked crust in the bottom of the pan, then the stuffed birds, adding salt and pepper and herbs, let them soak in butter and some flour for thickening, and then made the top crust. At the last minute she poured in cream through a little funnel at the top, and my dear, it was simply incredibly good. It's a southern speciality. Now it's time for lunch; let me make you some food."

With this Katherine Anne took me to her kitchen and out of the refrigerator came the most marvelous steaks; she knows what is good for you.

"I have them cut thick, because I think a steak ought to be thick. In Washington they call it Delmonico. It is very tender, but unfortunately also very expensive. But I can take the inexpensive part of meat and do quite a lot with it too."

I don't doubt it. Katherine Anne popped the steaks into her sizzling broiler and very soon they were on our plates. And exquisite.

"It will help to heal our bones," said Katherine Anne.

"Tell me, how did you make a living before your great success with *Ship of Fools*?"

"Since my first speech in 1934 at the American Women's Club in Paris, I have been lecturing all over the world. I talked mostly about the experiences of a writer. My way of writing has always been the same: before I sit down to write a story, I must know it by heart, and I write from memory. I believe in the conscientious, disciplined artist, the craftsman. It's a long and painful process."

"That makes me think of Paul Valéry," I said. "When he gave his lectures about poetry at the Collège de France, he once said to me: 'They think that in a few hours I can give them the recipe for writing poetry, while I myself have to tear it from my entrails.' "

"Valéry is the French writer I admire most and remember best, and I read him for refreshment quite often. I believed in him. He was so satisfactory, that wonderful clear mind of his that I loved."

Which you have too, dear Katherine Anne Porter. Add a pinch of wit, a dash of humor, and a soupçon of irony—plus your love and understanding of mankind. To know you, all one has to do is to read you, a revealing experience.

Conclusion

"A whole life . . . is terrifying and wondrous," exclaimed Elsa Triolet upon seeing a slide show of my color portraits at the Paris Musée d'Art Moderne during an exhibition in 1968. Almost thirty years had passed since my first slide show at Adrienne Monnier's bookshop. Once again writers and artists had come to see themselves: André Malraux, Henri Michaux, Michel Butor, Nathalie Sarraute, Vieira da Silva, Gilioli, and many others filed past the photographs on display.

The wonder was finding cherished faces in all the freshness of youth; the terror was in sometimes comparing them to more recent pictures that brought out the ravages of time. Yet some of my models had improved, their features more strongly modeled or more serene.

Today the portrait photographer has almost disappeared, seeing that there are hundreds of millions of amateurs. What does the amateur, in fact, photograph? I recall the visit of a friend, Maria, and her husband, Mario, a few years ago. They had decided to take a trip around the world, and when they finally arrived in Paris, they were exhausted. As Mario told me: "We've seen so much that everything is all mixed up in my

248

mind," but as a hunter brandishes his spoils, he handed me a hundred rolls of film and asked me to have them developed in my laboratory.

"Everything's there; you'll see!" he said triumphantly. Together we looked at the results. We saw Maria in front of the pyramids, Maria in front of a temple in India, Maria in front of the Kremlin, Maria on a beach in the Caribbean, Maria in front of a grotto in Turkey, Maria in front of a church in Spain, Maria, Maria, Maria.

Mario pulled a long face, for while Maria was perfectly recognizable on all the photographs, it was often difficult to make out the background against which she had been taken. "Don't be upset," I told him. "You have brought back a marvelous souvenir from your wonderful trip: a thousand copies of Maria."

In the hands of amateurs a camera is, first of all, a docile instrument that serves to photograph themselves, after which it is used to compose a diary in pictures. Millions of tourists roam the world every year, with camera in hand. In our consumer society, organized trips have replaced adventure. "Twelve countries in a week" advertises one of the big tourist agencies which organizes package tours. Everything is arranged beforehand: the countries, the hotels, the sites to visit—and all in record time. The harassed tourist has hardly a chance to sightsee; indeed, he is lucky if he finds a few minutes to press the button of his camera.

One day, at Orly airport, I encountered an elderly couple who had just landed.

"How marvelous," they exclaimed. "Finally in Frankfurt."

"But you're in Paris; you have just *come* from Frankfurt," said the tourist agent who was there to meet them. The husband made a fatalistic gesture.

"It doesn't matter; I have my camera. Once I get home, I'll see all the countries I've traveled through."

They left, bent under the weight of their baggage. In their case, as with millions of others, the photograph had substituted a pseudo-truth for the real world.

250   In its social function, the photograph today is a mass medium of prime importance, for nothing is as persuasive or as accessible to everyone. For a small number of photographers—and I am among them—a picture is far more than a mere means of giving information: by way of the camera, we express ourselves. A photographer is asked, not to create forms, but to reproduce them. In the hierarchy of artists he is closest to the translator, and a good translator must himself know how to write.

Selected
Iconography

PORTRAITS: WRITERS

France

Louis Aragon (1937, 1964), Colette Audry (1968), Claude Aveline (1939, 1967), Henri Barbusse (1935), Hervé Bazin (1961), Simone de Beauvoir (1948, 1970), Samuel Beckett (1964), André Breton (1938, 1965), Michel Butor (1966), Roger Caillois (1939, 1967), Jean Cassou (1939, 1965), Paul Claudel (1938), Jean Cocteau (1939), Colette (1938, 1954), Eugène Dabit (1935), Daniel-Rops (1960), Paul Desjardins (1938), Pierre Drieu La Rochelle (1934), Georges Duhamel (1938, 1956), Marguerite Duras (1965), Paul Eluard (1938), Léon-Paul Fargue (1939, 1948), Max-Pol Fouchet (1966), André Gide (1939), Jean Giono (1939, 1968), Jean Guéhenno (1935, 1967), Louis Guilloux (1971), Eugène Ionesco (1965, 1970, 1972), Michel Leiris (1966), Françoise Mallet-Joris (1965), André Malraux (1935, 1967, 1970), Félicien Marceau (1960), Gabriel Marcel (1965), François Mauriac (1938, 1967), André Maurois (1939, 1967), Albert Memmi (1968), Henri Michaux (1937, 1969, 1970), Adrienne Monnier (1935, 1953), Henry de Montherlant (1938), Paul Morand (1939), Paul Nizan (1939), Jean Paulhan (1937, 1964), Henri Pichette (1953), Jacques Prévert (1958), Raymond Queneau (1964), Alain Robbe-Grillet (1964, 1970), Christiane Rochefort (1964), Romain Rolland (1940), Jules Romains

251

(1939, 1967), Denis de Rougemont (1939, 1967), Claude Roy (1954), Françoise Sagan (1961), Saint-John Perse (1965, 1967), Nathalie Sarraute (1965), Jean-Paul Sartre (1939, 1968), Jean Schlumberger (1939, 1954), Claude Simon (1967), Philippe Soupault (1948), Jules Supervielle (1939, 1961), Henri Thomas (1939, 1968), Elsa Triolet (1939, 1964), Henri Troyat (1960, 1968), Tristan Tzara (1939), Paul Valéry (1939), Charles Vildrac (1939, 1957), Louise de Vilmorin (1962), Marguerite Yourcenar (1971)

Italy
Alberto Moravia (1963)

Spain
Rafael Alberti (1950, 1961), José Bergamin (1939), Leon Felipe (1952), José Ortega y Gasset (1939)

Cuba
Alejo Carpentier (1962), Nicolas Guillen (1952, 1965)

England
Kingsley Amis (1967), W. H. Auden (1963), Elizabeth Bowen (1939), Ivy Compton-Burnett (1959), Lawrence Durrell (1961), T. S. Eliot (1939), E. M. Forster (1935), Christopher Fry (1959), Graham Greene (1957), Pamela Hansford-Johnson (1959), Aldous Huxley (1935), Christopher Isherwood (1963), James Joyce (1938, 1939), Arthur Koestler (1939, 1967), Rosamund Lehmann (1959), Nancy Mitford (1960), Iris Murdoch (1959), J. B. Priestly (1959), Victoria (Vita) Sackville-West (1939), G. B. Shaw (1939), C. P. Snow (1959), Stephen Spender (1939, 1963), H. G. Wells (1939), Angus Wilson (1959), Virginia Woolf (1939)

Argentina
Adolfo Bioy (1943), Jorge Louis Borges (1943, 1952, 1971), Julio Cortazar (1967), Enrique Larreta (1943), Eduardo Mallea (1943), E. Martinez Estrada (1943), Manuel Mujica Lainez (1943), Victoria Ocampo (1939, 1964), Ernesto Sabato (1962)

Chile
Vincente Huidobro (1943), Pablo Neruda (1943, 1965, 1971)

Guatemala 253

Miguel Angel Asturias (1962, 1968, 1970)

United States
Sylvia Beach (1936, 1959), Erskine Caldwell (1959), Truman Capote
(1966), Mary McCarthy (1963, 1964), James Jones (1963, 1968), Robert Lowell (1964), Henry Miller (1960, 1961), Vladimir Nabokov
(1938, 1967), Katherine Anne Porter (1970), Philip Roth (1970), Cor-
nelius Ryan (1961), Irwin Shaw (1961), John Steinbeck (1961), William
Styron (1968), Thornton Wilder (1939, 1957), Tennessee Williams
(1959), Richard Wright (1951, 1958)

Canada
Mavis Gallant (1960), Anne Hebert (1955), Brian Moore (1957)

Switzerland
Friedrich Dürrenmatt (1961)

Germany
Walter Benjamin (1933, 1939), Bertolt Brecht (1935, 1954), Paul Celan (1965), Günther Grass (1972), Hermann Hesse (1962), Rolf Hoch-
huth (1968), Egon Erwin Kisch (1935), Heinrich Mann (1935), Stefan
Zweig (1939)

U.S.S.R.
Bella Akhmadulina (1965), Ilya Ehrenburg (1935), Yuri Kazakov
(1965), Boris Pasternak (1935), Andrei Voznesensky (1965), Yevgeny
Yevtushenko (1963).

Czechoslovakia
Vadlav Hável (1969), Karel Kosik (1969), Milan Kundera (1969)

Poland
Witold Gombrowicz (1968)

Israel
Martin Buber (1958), Gershom Scholem (1970)

Carlos Fuentes (1967), Octavio Paz (1962, 1971), Alfonso Reyes (1952)

PORTRAITS: PAINTERS, SCULPTORS, MUSICIANS

Pierre Bonnard (1947), Alexander Calder (1955), Pablo Casals (1958), Marc Chagall (1959), Salvador Dali (1967), Marcel Duchamp (1938, 1967), Max Ernst (1968), Alberto Giacometti (1965), Frida Kahlo (1952), Oskar Kokoschka (1967), Alfredo Lam (1968), Le Corbusier (1961), Henri Matisse (1948), Darius Milhaud (1958, 1966), Henry Moore (1964), Charles Munch (1968), José Clemente Orozco (1952), Man Ray (1967), Diego Rivera (1952), Vieira da Silva (1968), David Alfaro Siqueiros (1952), Graham Sutherland (1963, 1967), Rufino Tamayo (1952)

PHOTO-STORIES

Argentina (1943, 1952), Austria (1935, 1964), Bolivia (1948), Canada (1949, 1969), Chile (1944), Czechoslovakia (1969), Ecuador (1947), England (1935, 1971), France (1933, 1971), Germany (1931, 1968), Hong Kong (1970), Israel (1971), Japan (1970), Mexico (1950, 1952), Paraguay (1945), Peru (1948), Switzerland (1938, 1967), United States (1949, 1970), Uruguay (1951)

ARTS

Pre-Columbian Mexico: Tlatilco, Olmec, Aztec, Mayan, Toltec, Gulf coast, Western coast, and Zapotecan civilizations

Peru: Chimu civilization

Colonial: Paraguay, Argentina, Ecuador, and Mexico

Europe: Italy and France

Index

255